Esquire Handbook
for Hosts

Esquire Handbook for Hosts

THE ORIGINAL '50s GUIDE FOR

THE SOPHISTICATED MAN

EDITED BY PETER HOWARTH

Thorsons

Thorsons
An Imprint of HarperCollins*Publishers*
77–85 Fulham Palace Road,
Hammersmith, London W6 8JB

The Thorsons website address is: www.thorsons.com

First Published by Frederick Muller Ltd., 1954
Published by Thorsons 1999

10 9 8 7 6 5 4 3 2 1

A catalogue record for this book
is available from the British Library

ISBN 0 7225 3902 9

Printed and bound in Great Britain by
Woolnoughs Bookbinding Ltd, Irthlingborough, Northants

Contents

The Host At Home

The first and foremost thing to be said about the perfect host is – he doesn't exist.

The perfect host makes every guest feel like a guest-of-honour, but he fusses over no one, exploits no one, spends no more time with one than another.

He makes even the dullest guest feel witty, a shining light among pleasant and appreciative companions, but he does not appear to draw anyone out. He is a witty fellow himself, but not so anyone can notice his wit as such; his wit is catalytic, somehow, making everyone else feel good.

He provides good food, good drink, good company – but he makes no point of any of them. The next drink materialises at the very moment when his guest notices that his glass is empty (not before, ostentatiously; not after, apologetically). The next conversational group moves onto the horizon at the very moment when the guests have begun to run down on their current topic (not in mid-discussion, frustratingly; not in the final stages of bore-dom, desperately).

He anticipates his guest's every need and wish, but not obtrusively; he makes it seem that he is prompted by his own desires. He is alert, but he appears relaxed.

All these things are engineered, but so subtly so naturally, that no one ever thinks 'What a good host,' only 'What a good time I had.'

The perfect host, you see, is a wraith; no man is that perfect. And, ironi-cally, the man who tries hardest misses by the biggest margin. He urges, he pounces, he interrupts, he is a host on horseback. He also worries, and his nervousness is catching. Even the too-casual host, scourge that he is, is apt to be better off than the E-for-Effort host. He forces each guest to be his own host; he relaxes so much that he folds up onto the bed into the back room; but one person, at least, has a good time at his party: he does.

The struggle for perfection, then, contain the seeds of its own failure. And real (rather than apparent) relaxation is a failure at the outset. With a little attention to detail, and a little practice, you can land somewhere in between. You will have a maximum of good moments, a minimum of bad ones.

ETIQUETTE REFRESHER

Modern etiquette might better be termed 'manners', and thus be stripped of its stuffy implications; for it is simply a code of conduct, regularly revised in keeping with the spirit of the times, designed to make social living more pleasant for all concerned. If you are guided by a consideration for others, you need no rule books.

One of the easiest things to be awkward about is the matter of:

INTRODUCTIONS

It is seldom necessary or even desirable to introduce people casually encountered in public places. Under no circumstances is it advisable to make an introduction if it involves scrambling about and making everyone concerned uncomfortable – as in a restaurant where getting to your feet would involve pushing the table about and stepping into the aisle. It would, it seems to us, be preferable by far to journey through life anonymously.

In most of our larger cities, the business of introducing people has been treated with refreshing common sense. Only at house parties, at small dinner parties and similar functions is it considered essential, and then the introduction is made in the simplest possible form. All of the 'May I presents' have gone by the board in favour of the more laconic but wholly courteous, 'Miss Struthers, Mr Arbuthnot'.

INVITATIONS

The matter of issuing formal invitations is another bugbear. Purveyors of engraving have fostered the idea that we should announce, in courtly language and suitable, hand-cut typography, the most casual of celebrations, the most ordinary of comings or goings. As a matter of fact, the engraved invitation is nothing but a nuisance and may be dispensed with for anything short of weddings, large dances or gargantuan dinner parties. For less formal entertaining, upon the part of a man, the calling card may be used. Simply write the date, time and nature of the occasion in the corner in longhand.

If you receive such an invitation, no reply is really needed. However, in the case of a small dinner or dance an RSVP may be included. The form for replying is equally simple. Just grasp one of your own cards and, writing in the date for which you have been invited, add a phrase like 'With pleasure'.

And even this effortless method has been largely supplanted – for small and informal entertaining – by the telephone, the telegraph or just plain word of mouth. Let mutual convenience be your guide in issuing invitations; in answering, follow the same form as the invitation itself, be it 3rd person formal engraved or 'come up and see us'.

SHOULD YOU ASK HER IN?

The occasions upon which a man really requires manners, and upon which manners actually show themselves, usually have to do with entertaining women who, for one reason or another, are on their own, and who the man does not know very well. A well-chaperoned young woman you may ask in for a night cap, whereas a girl living by herself should not be similarly importuned by you. It may all seem very unreasonable but experience will teach you that there's a great deal to be gained in the long run out of walking softly.

After all, in a world where men are popularly supposed to spend their waking hours in devising new methods of making illicit overtures – God knows when they work! – it is a sound idea to employ what manners you can marshal, be your intentions never so overt. If, on the other hand, you are completely innocent of anything beyond a desire to dine in pleasant company, decent manners will save you the trouble of spending valuable time in allaying unfounded suspicion.

Admitting that the gag: 'Mother, what is a chaperone?' has a certain humorous validity, it is well known that the species has managed to persist in the face of all opposition. The present-day chaperone remains the staunch prop of outward virtue and the bachelor's bane.

As a bachelor, you will at least occasionally crave female companionship and, at least occasionally, you will have no ulterior motive. Admittedly it is difficult to convince some women of this. That a man carries neither the marriage nor the seduction of a given female in the back of his mind is quite incomprehensible to them. What, then, can be done?

Our own tendency is toward ecleticism. Rather than to postulate a set of rules of conduct, we incline to judge each case on its, or her, merits. Size up your wench, then go ahead.

Let us first consider that it is your wish to entertain a business woman; perhaps she is a buyer, a customer of yours, possibly she is an advertising copywriter or maybe she is simply somebody's stenographer. In any case she is a female who has had some actual contact with the workaday world and therefore not one to be unduly impressed with your delicate observance of the more threadbare conventions.

If your acquaintance with this admirable member of her sex is slight or your entertainment offered for business rather than purely social reasons, there is but one course open to you: take her to a public place for luncheon, dinner or the theatre, escort her home and let it go at that. Public entertainment is governed largely by common sense. You may take anyone to tea, dinner or the theatre, but if you want to go on in the small hours of the morning to notoriously crime-ridden area of town, or to some rather dubious night club, you'd best make certain of the degree of broadmindedness enjoyed by the lady and her family. Shotgun weddings may be out of fashion but a Model 'T' parent can still make life pretty uncomfortable for you.

If, on the other hand, you know the girl well and if, better still, she has been given no reason to believe that you mean to work your wicked will upon her once the opportunity presents itself, there is no reason on earth why you should not ask her to your apartment for a cocktail or a meal or even to look at your etchings, should you chance to have any. All of the delicious shudders and most of the social taboos have been eliminated from the once daring adventure of 'visiting a bachelor in his rooms', at least so far as adults are concerned.

It is intended as no reflection upon the business woman that she may be treated somewhat less conventionally than, say, a sub-debutante; rather it is a compliment. No modern woman in her right mind and past the age of consent wishes to preserve the ancient fiction of her fragility in the face of a practical world, and any additional consideration offered the sub-deb is in the nature of a sop to her maternal parent and not as a pretty gesture in the general direction of the girl.

If you wish to entertain so young a girl or one who has received an immoderate amount of sheltering, you may be forced to employ chaperonage of one variety or another. Conventionally, a chaperone should be a married woman, yet it can cause more gossip for you to harbour a young married woman in your rooms, than by having a young girl up alone. Perhaps the greatest convenience a bachelor can have is a sister who will permit herself to be pressed into service. For some reason or other no one seems to suspect the motives of a man whose sister habitually acts as chaperone-cum-hostess for him. It is not, you will recall, your own lack of morals but the whisper of the scandalmonger that stimulates you to all this effort in behalf of a girl's mother.

Again, in the case of young girls, it is both sensible and safe to ask them to your apartment in groups of three of more. This practice provides you with a variety of automatic, self-loading chaperones, inexpensive to operate and maintain and involving no additional obligation on your part. Even if your affections happen to be centred upon one of your guests and one alone, you have provided her with more than adequate protection, for unless a girl is of sub-normal intelligence she will never permit her contemporaries to have anything on her. As for you, your hands, metaphorically, are tied.

If you go in for dinner parties you need not worry overmuch about violating conventions. There is safety in numbers. Nevertheless, and despite all that has been written about the reaction toward social conservation of the rising generation, it is still the part of discretion to keep a weather eye on the drinking and see to it that your younger guests do not imbibe too freely. This is a matter of protection, not parsimony; there is small pleasure to be derived from finding yourself with an eighteen-year-old passout on your hands.

Should you be so fortunate as to have a country place of your own, you may entertain there quite as freely as you might were you married. Of course, if you run to week-end house parties you'll require a married couple to be among those present, but that should work no hardship if you pick them with reasonable care and a working knowledge of their habits. If, on the other hand, your country place consists of a shack in the woods minus adequate bedroom facilities, you'd be wiser to confine yourself to entertainment which does not involve putting your guests up overnight.

DINING WITHOUT PAIN

Formal dinners, in any save great households, are an anachronism. Very few people, nowadays, are equipped to give them, and if there is any doubt at all in your mind about the ability of your own household to carry off one of these oppressive functions, you may be sure that you'd best not attempt it. A more modest affair, on the other hand, is often a great success.

Possibly the most important thing to avoid, in giving a dinner, is the appearance of pretentiousness. Do not attempt anything that is beyond the ordinary limitations of your establishment. If the local handy man claims to be able to double up as a butler or footman, be certain that he is going to get away with it. Remember it's a hundred to one hot that he won't.

And if, as is more likely, the dinner is completely in your own hands, do your serving from the sideboard or at the table, 'family style,' or retreat completely to a buffet supper.

You can strain your house to the bursting point and yet bring off a buffet supper successfully. Simply move the dining-room chairs back against the wall, set out several hot dishes and a cold joint or two on the dining-room table and your problem is solved. What carving there is to do is best accomplished beforehand in the kitchen, and your most important task during the event will be that of removing the empty or partially emptied plates before your guests have a change either to step on them or sit in them.

At a small dinner the problem of whom to invite is a serious one. You do not, in a group of eight, want four noisy people and four quiet ones. A single talker, provided he is not a pedant or a bore or both should be sufficient. Do not ask all your clever friends to one dinner and the dull ones to another. Nothing annoys a clever man or woman more than a second one; and even the conversationally dull are not complimented at being grouped with their peers. If you are giving a dinner for a business associate of some importance, let him be important. He will appreciate it.

After dinner, you can take refuge in bridge, backgammon or games. Of these latter be careful, for many a dinner guest resents being asked to perform feats of memory or erudition on a full stomach. There is always conversation or music upon which to fall back, provided your guests are equipped to perform creditably in either of these arts. The tactful host will be certain of the capacities of his guests or will provide them with more innocent diversion.

BLUEPRINT FOR A COCKTAIL PARTY

THE SUMMONSES – Printed, penned or phoned, can be sizeable card or folder, plain or decorated, formal or bearing genial salutations. Whatever for it takes, it should state day, time (usually 4–6 or 5–7), and place, with mention of cocktails. And don't forget RSVP if you care. Invitations should be issued one to two weeks in advance.

POPULATION ESTIMATE – To be on the safe side, invite ten or twenty percent more people than you want to attend. Or, if you're operating without RSVP's, count on about 70% of the crowd putting in an appearance. One sound theory says that the party should either be small enough so everyone can be seated or large enough so that the standees won't fell embarrassed.

GLASSWARE – You need at least two to a customer of shapes and sizes required by the pouring program: 3 oz. cocktail stemmers (busiest), 10oz. highball glasses (close competitors), 2 oz. V-glasses for sherry, Old Fashioned glasses (if you're serving that drink), champagne glasses if festivity is the order of the day.

BEVERAGE SUPPLIES – Three drinks per person is a fair allowance. You compute the bottles without calculus if you know your clue numbers. Basic 18 is the number of jiggers (1oz. each) that a spirit bottle (25.6 oz.) will pour. Translated, it means 17 Martinis per bottle of gin, 18 Daiquiris per bottle of rum, 17 Manhattans or Old Fashioneds per bottle of whisky. If brandy or Scotch highballs are of 1 jigger strength, 17 washes up the bottle.

But let's be larger-minded, tripling our jiggers to 51 and throwing away the spare, which would probably be accounted for by spillage anyhow. Now our yardstick is 50 drinks from 3 bottles – offering an easy jump to 200 drinks from 1 case. But the vermouths, dry for the Martinis and sweet for the Manhattans, are still to be reckoned. They operate at half-jigger speed: 34 cocktails (17 doubled) to the bottle. Fifty cocktails therefore mean 1 bottle of vermouth, along with the 3 bottles of liquor; and the case job of 200 could require 6 vermouth bottles.

Sherry deals are 2 oz., a dozen to the bottle, which leaves a small residue providing a starter on the next glass; so count 25 for 2 bottles. Similarly 2 bottles of liquor will yield 25 highballs of 2oz. strength. (More appropriate for a stag affair than a mixed party.) Champagne, straight or cocktailed, is 6–9 to the bottle.

At a cocktail party, it's a safe bet to offer:

1 standard cocktail (Martini, Manhattan or Old Fashioned)

1 other cocktail, either standard or more fanciful

Whisky and soda, for the long drinkers

An aperitif, for the mild drinkers (sherry or Dubonnet)

A non-alcoholic drink, for the wagon-riders.

Ice – More than you could expect of your refrigerator. If you live in a city, phone a cube service; in the country, your ice company will oblige. Shakers and mixing glasses require cracked ice.

Flowers – By all means, but vases where they won't be knocked over.

Cigarettes – Invitingly stood up in shot glasses in many strategic spots. Ash trays everywhere. Matches, table lighters.

Canapés – Single-mouthful propositions, avoiding the necessity of individual plates which men hate to be encumbered with.

CONFUSION CONTROL

If you live in an apartment house, you can save yourself a lot of running every time the bell rings, if you leave the front door open. The parking of coats and hats will be simplified if guests, as they enter, can see at a glance where they are to lay their things. Perhaps on tables (or borrowed hat racks) by the door – or place right out in the hall – if you can trust your neighbours! If coats are to be put in bedrooms, have signs conspicuously displayed bearing arrows, one reading 'Boys,' the other 'Girls'. If your party is large and formal, then, of course you will hire a checker. But if you indulge in such swank, then you're probably going to put yourself in the hands of professionals – caterers, florists and such – and you won't need these helps.

All persons assisting in the operation of this party have definite assignments. Somebody is stationed near the door to greet incomers and start the introductions. Somebody has the job of scouting for empty glasses and whisking them out to the kitchen, where they are promptly washed and put back into service; otherwise the party might get stalled by glass shortage, a calamity exceeded only by that of running out of liquor. Those in charge of pouring have their work simplified for them by fruit juices already squeezed, slices and peels neatly dished, and Martini and Manhattan mixtures prepared in advance or, for convenience, bought bottled. The cracked ice isn't soupy; and cubes aren't left melting in glasses destined for highballs. Shaker productions are presented while still cloudy and foam-edged. To ease congestion at the bar, trays of drinks are passed around. Somebody musical is coaxed to the piano. Songs are joined in. Everybody is of the opinion that it's a swell party. Even its planner contrives to smile through his cares.

What the Well-Dressed Host Will Wear

Granting that you are a bachelor and not a hermit, that you are going to entertain pretty regularly in the apartment and not spend all of your time prowling after a pair of nylon legs, here are a few simple suggestions on what to wear when the friends come around for a few drinks. Wise ones will be as much concerned about their clothes as the amount of vermouth in the Martinis and the composition of the hors d'oeuvers.

Unless you've called in outside assistance, you're going to be doing a few chores, so keep coolness and comfort in mind and wear the lightweight worsted evening trousers of midnight blue with a single braid down each side. The word comfort has real meaning when you're wearing black ribbed nylon socks and patent leather or black suede pumps. The latter, with bright red linings, are gaining favour of late; they won't crack over the instep and they always look well-groomed after a brief brushing.

There is about as much leeway in the choice jackets as there is in liquors. Only a few are just right. Tops on the preferred jacket list is the double-chested type of dark maroon velveteen. A modern version of the smoking jacket, it has self-faced braid lapels and four buttons covered with the same fabric as that of the jacket. Some hosts like the same jacket in bright scarlet and others go for blue velvet or velveteen. The main idea is that the host should not only be dressed adequately but should be distinguishable from the rest of the guests who are put at ease by this home-only type of outfit.

If you are one who sticks to the tried and true, your double-chested dinner jacket of the same lightweight midnight blue fabric as the dress trousers is always in good taste. In fact, the lustrous satin facings on the lapels will even give an added formal gleam to your appearance.

A boutonniere is an extra touch of style that doesn't take too much thinking. Wear a white carnation for the dark red jacket and a red carnation for midnight blues.

Finally, unfold a white linen handkerchief and hold it at the centre, allowing the points to hang irregularly. Fold it in half so that the centre point falls just below the corner points and tuck it casually into the chest pocket with the centre point side toward the body. One corner hanging out like a rabbit's ear or precise arrangement of the points is exactly what you don't want, so keep it casual.

Recently, hosts also have been wearing the television coat – a loose-fitting, finger-tip length garment with large pockets. It comes in figured foulard or lightweight flannel.

For a cocktail party, prior to a dinner out, a bachelor's business suit, in blue or grey, fills all requirements. Wide-spread collars or tabs on your white shirt dictate the knot of a modestly patterned tie. The former takes a Windsor and the latter is best with a four-in-hand.

While combining breakfast and lunch into brunch, it is also astute to combine the right casual, informal clothes. Assuming that you had enough sleep and have a reasonably clear head, you'll probably select a pair of the old reliable grey-flannel slacks and a tweed sports jacket. An Oxford shirt, bow-tie or four-in-hand, and comfortable shoes like loafers or moccasins complete the brunch outfit for Autumn, Winter and Spring.

When the sun begins to spend most of its time on this side of the planet, especially during the very warm summery days, our bachelor friend will replace the light tweed jacket with a linen blazer; the flannel slacks will give way to lighter weight gabardine.

A final word: The objective behind all of this is not to make you into a fashion plate, but rather to give you an opportunity to be a distinctive host with a plate full of canapés in one hand and a fair lass on your arm, with not a single clothes-conscious moment. That's the point, gentlemen: dress your part.

Eat

The World's Best Chefs Wear Pants

'All human history attests
That happiness for man – the hungry sinner! –
Since Eve ate apples, much depends on dinner.'
– Byron

The world's greatest cooks are men. Since the beginning of time, he-men have always prepared the savoury dishes that caress the palates of epicures of every nation.

Some have taken up the culinary art as a new twist on the old 'come-see-my-etchings' routine. Some have come to the kitchen out of necessity: even bachelors must eat. But all have remained to reap the pleasures from (and the praises for) good food thoughtfully prepared.

For the 'emergency' cook whose kitchen prowess begins and ends with frying an egg, but who would like to be prepared for some pleasant emergency – say a snow-stranded damsel with an appetite...For the man who knows how to prepare only one dish well, and is beginning to notice that friends and wooed-one pale at the mention of spaghetti...For the man who is overcome by righteous rage at the thought of women's magazine salads...For every man, everywhere, who appreciates fine food...For gourmet and gourmand alike, Esquire has assembled this guide. 'Read, mark, learn and inwardly digest' and you'll emerge as a chef supreme and wine connoisseur who can spar with the smuggest sommelier.

You won't find doily tea-room fare here: no radish roses, no menus designed for their low calorie content. Esquire had concentrated on food of, for and by MEN. Nor will you find charts of how long to roast lamb or how to make an apple pie, we recommend that you have a standard, womanly cookbook for reference in such routine matters, for this book is concerned not with the kind of food you can get anywhere but with unusual dishes. Esquire suspects that you'll prove nothing (and improve nothing) if you compete with three-meals-a-day cooks on their own territory. So here are the little-known recipes of internationally famous chefs, the unexpected touches which transform an ordinary food into an extraordinary dinner, the super dishes that will establish your reputation as a cook even if you never learn to bake a cake or disguise a left-over.

'Be different, host-cook, and let he who will forever serve fried chicken.'

How to use this book

Read the book through first for ideas, pick out the dishes which most appeal to you, then try the recipes on yourself, so you'll be confident and assured when the time comes to perform for an audience. And if you rank as a rank beginner, you may need this basic dope even before you start to read and practice.

Boiling is cooking in water at a temperature of 212 degrees Fahrenheit; simmering is cooking in water at a temperature of 180 to 210 degrees Fahrenheit, or below the boiling point of water; stewing is simmering in very small amount of liquid for a long time; streaming is cooking in the steam generated by a small amount of boiling water in the vessel. Broiling, or grilling, is cooking over or under direct heat; pan broiling is cooking in a pan greased only enough to prevent the food in it from sticking. Baking and roasting are practically the same – cooking in the oven at various temperatures required by the food you are cooking. Frying is cooking in a bath of hot fat, while sautéing is done in a small quantity of fat; fricasseeing is a combination of sautéing with stewing or steaming.

DON'T 'IMPROVE' ON THE RECIPES, at least at first. On the first time around, we suggest that you follow the recipes exactly. If 1 tablespoon of flour is called for, measure exactly 1 level tablespoonful. If 'flour to thicken' is the order, note the precise amount required so you'll have a starting point for future experiments. Then, when your first test shows you what the recipe was working toward, you're in a better position to...

ADD A TOUCH OF IMAGINATION, LATER – it's like painting. Matisse wouldn't have got anywhere if he hadn't sat those long hours in the Louvre copying Delacroix. The real artist adds his own interpretation to the matter at hand; and if the métier is the kitchen range, his dash of this or that is as individual as the painter's brush stroke. So learn the rules, and then throw them away, one at a time. Only then can you take the real creator's pride in your dish and put it out as a little thing of your own.

Of course, let's face it, in the first rush of inspiration you're apt to court failure, grand or small. Until you've cornered that major ingredient of good cookery – experience – things don't always come out the way you plan them:

...But in case of failure you can always (a) have another pitcher of Martinis, (b) call the nearest caterer, or (c) exit, laughing. But whatever you do, spare yourself and your guests that other Great Fault of women cooks: apologizin' and a-fussin'.

But, whether paying strict attention to a recipe or cooking freehand...

USE YOUR COMMON SENSE – no good cook follows a recipe slavishly. A man takes to the stove because he is interested in cooking, therefore he has long been interested in eating and therefore he starts six lengths in front of the average female. A vague direction like 'season to taste' makes more sense to him than 'add 1 teaspoon salt'. We suspect that your chance of error lies in the other, casual direction – but don't say we didn't warn you: a recipe is a guide, not a law.

PLAN EVERYTHING WELL IN ADVANCE: don't trust to luck or to supplies-on-hand. Go over your menu and wine list carefully, check to make sure you have everything you need in the way of equipment and supplies, then you can confidently attend to your guests with no time out for worrying.

Best bet is to do your planning on paper, too. To a host who wants his cooking to appear effortless, *memory is a poor substitute for schedules and shopping lists*:

Do all of your table-setting and as much as possible of your cooking before your guests arrive, so you won't have to rush around during the cocktail period. A written time schedule is a big help, if only because such a carefully-thought-out plan is a constant reassurance that you haven't forgotten anything. As you'll learn for yourself, the first time you discover your prize salad or your special dessert still in the refrigerator on the morning after –

only because you forgot to serve it — it doesn't pay to become infatuated with the taste of your own martinis unless you have a concealed list to do your thinking for you.

REMEMBER THE SAYING ABOUT TOO MANY COOKS — it's true: too many cooks not only get in your hair but may spoil your fare. Particularly in the early stages of your cooking experience, onlookers will rattle you; and if they insist upon rattling pots and pans as well, you'll wish you'd stood in the restaurant set.

So if you can get away with it, keep your gallery out of the galley. A display of temperament might work; a fresh supply of cocktails set out as far as possible from the cookstove is more certain to leave you a clear field in the food department.

If your best efforts fail and your busybody guests prevail, you can either (a) crowd them into a kitchen corner, (b) force this book into their hands, to keep them occupied or (c) make a point of bumping into them at every turn, until they suspect that they're in the way. But, whatever you do, *don't let them help*. Let a woman fix so much as a cracker and she'll soon take over.

Whose hobby *is* this, anyway?

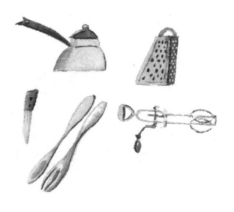

Equipment

PANS MAKE THE MAN EFFICIENT

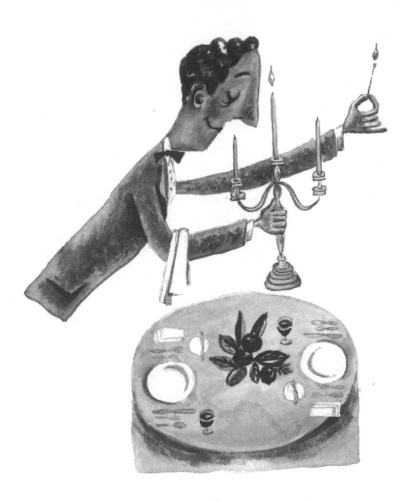

A man's kitchenette should contain the following necessary utensils: a kettle, a set of saucepans – preferably with long handles, a frying pan, a roasting pan, a double boiler, at least one earthenware casserole, a wire sieve, a wire salad basket, an egg beater, mixing bowls, three kitchen knives, a small wooden chopping board, a vegetable brush, a wooden spoon and fork, a spatula, a long fork, a grater, a funnel, a pepper mill, a pair of scissors, a measure, a basting spoon, a coffee-pot, a teapot and a wooden salad bowl. If your oven has no heat control, by all means get an oven thermometer. And even if it does have a broiler rack, you may want a sizzle platter, which both broils and serves such foods as steaks and chops. Individual casseroles are nice to have, for soup-serving as well as miscellaneous cooking. A pressure cooker is helpful for vegetables; you'll want a potato masher or a good mill for potatoes, etc. Gadgets galore – from onion-chopper to wire whisks – will ease your course; and of course you'll want a good can opener. You'll save on temper, too, if you latch on to one of the new openers made to handle vacuum-jars. If you go in for electrical appliances, a good toaster, a waffle iron and a coffee-maker that does its work at the table make a good kick-off.

Then, depending on the tack your cooking takes, you may add special equipment: skewers for shish kebab, say, or an alcohol-flame chafing dish for almost anything dressy. You may need a deep-fry pan and basket; rolling pin, pastry board, baking pans; special moulds for baba au rum or the like; small, shallow frying pans for crêpes Suzette; even an omelette pan.

Ample equipment and the best, is a pleasure to work with, but like the good photographer who can make salon pictures even with a box camera, the good cook can turn out gourmet viands on a hotel hot plate.

If you're limited in the pots and pans department, DO THE BEST YOU CAN WITH WHAT YOU HAVE...and if your space is limited, MAKE YOUR EQUIPMENT DO DOUBLE DUTY.

Your casserole can double as a stewpan. A small saucepan floated in a larger one makes a double boiler, a pint bottle can substitute for a measuring cup, a frying pan can be used as an oven dish and so on. Be wise...improvise!

When it comes to table equipment, you'll probably want service for 6 or 8. We suggest you go in for....

MODERN DESIGN – modern china and linens were made for men: simple and striking they are utterly devoid of pink rosebuds and fancy decoration. Your tablecloth or runners will probably be in solid colour linen – wine, grey, bright blue or rust being the most popular. These may have contrasting borders, or your monogram in big bold letters. For brunch or very informal entertaining, you might invest in some bright coloured cellophane mats, or the new cork mats, neither of which ever have to go near a laundry!

Your china will be plain white or grey, with block initials or a modern striped border, and your silverware will be decidedly streamlined.

PEASANT DESIGN – this allows a lot of latitude. You may use gay Czechoslovakian linen cloths in raucous plaids or checks, or rough cottons that look like dish towels. Your china may be Mexican pottery, California pottery in vivid sun-drenched colours or French Provençal or Italian pottery, really charming and unbelievably hardy. With this you might use coloured glassware – effective and inexpensive.

Allow yourself such whimsies as wooden-handled cutlery or salad forks with bright painted handles. Have a large, impressive wooden salad bowl, and lots of copper utensils. Don't be afraid to use colour lavishly at your table: it has a great brightening effect.

As for EQUIPPING YOUR SHELVES here are some of the staples and condiments you'll want to keep on hand at all times: butter, flour, sugar, salt, pepper, onions, oil, vinegar, baking powder, gelatine, Parmesan cheese, coffee and tea, cocoa, mustard, ketchup, Worcestershire sauce, anchovy sauce, Hungarian paprika, curry powder, capers, bay leaf, garlic, cloves, vanilla, caraway seeds, raisins, rice, macaroni, black peppercorn, nutmeg, prunes, brown sugar and arrowroot. The major wines and liqueurs used for cooking are: Chablis, Claret, Marsala, Sherry and Maraschino.

In addition, try always to have SOMETHING TO FALL BACK ON...

Just in case you ever come down with unexpected guests (or with the sort of hangover that knocks out your going-to-market plans), keep a supply of canned goods at home: soup, vegetables, fish, meat, a pudding or two, fruits, condensed milk. Pick out a favourite quick dish – rarebit, omelette, corn-beef-hash-with-poached-egg or what you will – then make sure that you always have the necessary ingredients on tap. If you keep a close watch on your 'emergency shelf,' and make a point of replacing each item you use, your hospitality needn't be a sometimes thing.

How to Serve

WHEN YOU PUT YOUR
BEST FOOT FORWARD

Your kitchen-conquest will go for naught if you fluff the follow-through.

Attractive, knowing service makes good food taste superb. Even indifferent fare takes on an Epicurean air if it's set forth in the proper setting. So don't miss any of the tricks which weave an atmosphere of good living around your dining table. For instance...

PUT A LIGHT IN HER EYES – but not the kind that comes through the courtesy of Mr. Edison. Candlelight is perfect for mood-setting and food-abetting. Have enough candles to eliminate the Braille system of eating, but not so many as to brighten the corner where you're not. See that the candle tops are above eye level, and her eyes will centre on you – and your magnificent food. She'll say 'This is all so beautiful' – and *mean* it!

GIVE HER MUSIC, MAESTRO, PLEASE – make it soft music, background music, the unobtrusive kind of music that stimulates rather than irritates conversation (and digestive juices). Thus you'll have to put your jazz collection aside during the dinner hour, and even your favourite symphonies if they're by Shostakovich. Play instead a quiet tone poem by Debussy, a stack of gypsy-violin recordings. Note the notes' relaxing effect on yourself as well as on your guests!

ACT AS THOUGH YOU HAD 10 SERVANTS – your guests know you cooked their dinner, and they're already impressed with your talent or your courage, as the case may be. So you needn't keep reminding them of your chef role by hopping up and down, running back and forth between table and kitchen, during dinner. There could be no other point in such nerve-wracking antics, for it's a simple matter to arrange things so that 'Dinner is Served' means for cook-host as well as for the guests.

Plan a menu of minimum courses so that everything can be either on the table or on the sideboard or serving table before you announce dinner; make full use of your chafing dish if it's necessary to keep one course warm while another has the floor. Use a dressed-up 'family style' of service, with food for second helpings left on the table rather than returned to the kitchen after the first time around. Use trays for clearing the table, bringing in the dessert and coffee. And you'll find that you can play the lord of the manor at the head of the table, undisturbed by kitchen-calls, even if you are the cook.

AND DON'T NEGLECT THE LITTLE THINGS – the newly polished silver, the sparkling glassware, the crackling (non-smoking) fire in the grate, the cigarettes at each place, the heated dinner plates – all the little things combine to make a big thing of your food and wine. The atmosphere can be varied according to the menu – spaghetti might call for chequered tablecloth and operatic arias, while coq au vin might inspire the full formal treatment – but 'atmosphere' it must be if you would give your dinner the showcase it deserves. 'Showcase' is right: the proof of your pudding is in the way you present it. When you put your best food forward, remember...

IT ALL BOILS DOWN TO SHOWMANSHIP!

Canapés

NIBBLE WHILE YOU SIP

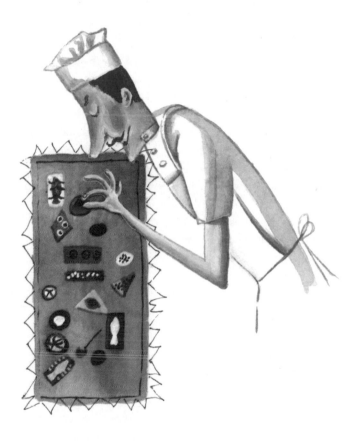

Everything from potato chip to caviar is nibbled in the name of canapé, so the host who would complement his cocktails (and draw compliments from his guests) need be inhibited by only one rule: the titbit served to whet appetites should not dampen the dinner to come. That is, your canapés should neither foreshadow flavours to be featured at dinner, nor take the appreciative edge off your guests' appetites. Eliminate tomato canapés if tomato sauce is on the dinner menu, scorn a filling cheese if a heavy dinner is en route, and then you're on your own. For if there's any course which courts imagination, it's this prelude to dining.

After you've tried the cocktail-accompaniments below, branch out: soften your favourite cheese with beer, or mash an avocado with onion and Tabasco...sample the 1001 cocktail crackers on the market...jazz up a bottled mayonnaise with all the condiments in the pantry, then offer dip-privileges with crisp raw vegetables...arm yourself with a can-opener and explore the epicure-shop shelves: miniature artichokes, all the pates, shrimps, anchovies, little sausages, beefs, mushrooms, devilled ham, tongue, pastes and spreads.

With a little experimentation, you'll soon develop a canapé repertoire equal to any occasion: from the cream-cheese-and-olive-type that goes with sherry flips, chaperoned meetings and your 'I can't-think-of-you-as-an-undergraduate' line...to the pickled-herring-on-sea-biscuit-type which supports your virile-bachelor, not-prepared-for-female-callers pose.

CANAPÉ MARGUERY

Take four pieces of toast, cook with sweet butter until crisp. Chop together one hard-boiled egg, six filets of anchovies, half a green pepper, one peeled tomato, and as much tuna fish as about the weight of an egg, and spread this mixture flat on top of the toast. Add a spoonful of Russian dressing (which is composed of mayonnaise and chilli sauce). Garnish with several drops of Worcestershire sauce, serve immediately.

HAM AND CHEESE ROLL

Take thin slices of ham, spread with mixture of Roquefort and cream cheese. Roll, fasten with toothpicks, place in refrigerator to chill until firm enough to slice. Slice fresh tomatoes, cut bread circles the same size as the slices. Toast the bread discs, butter, spread thickly with mayonnaise and place a tomato slice on top of each toast disc. Cut ham and cheese roll in thin slices and place one on top of each tomato slice. Sure-fire hit.

OLIVES ROLLED IN BACON

Take large olives stuffed with pimento and roll in a slice of lean bacon. Secure with toothpick and bake in a hot oven

OYSTERS AND MUSHROOMS

Take a fresh oyster and place in a large mushroom that has been peeled. Dip in olive oil or butter, sprinkle with salt, pepper, paprika and a dash of celery salt. Then place under a hot grill. Serve on half the oyster shell or a piece of thin toast.

PATÉ (EL BORRACHO)

1lb of butter
1 onion chopped
4oz of lard
1 jigger of sherry
1 bay leaf
salt and pepper
dash of red pepper
1 jigger of brandy
8oz of calf's liver, diced
(soak liver 24 hrs. in cold water)

Brown meat in fat; remove, and sauté onions with 8oz of butter, 4oz of lard and a jigger of sherry. Combine meat, bay leaf and seasonings. Mix thoroughly all together and let it simmer slowly for ten minutes. Then strain through cheese cloth or fine wire strainer. Now mix in the remaining butter and jigger of brandy. Place this in a mould and cover the top with a few tablespoonfuls of clear dissolved gelatine. Put into refrigerator and chill until firm. Serve on hot toasted squares, or crackers. Serves eight.

PETITE RAREBITS

Grate a half pound Swiss cheese and a half pound cheddar cheese, mix with the yolks of two eggs and one cup of rich cream. Spread on crackers or toast cut in rounds. Broil under a hot grill and, before serving, sprinkle with paprika.

PICKLE DILLIES

Use a small-mouthed glass to cut circular pieces of bread. Lay one or two slices of dill pickle on each bread circle, then sprinkle liberally with grated cheese. Bake in the oven until cheese melts. Serve hot.

PIGS IN CLOVER

Wrap a slice of lean bacon around a large oyster. Sprinkle with salt and pepper, paprika and garlic salt. Secure with a toothpick, place under a hot grill and serve when bacon is done.

SOUP SANDWICHES OR CANAPÉS

Combine and mix thoroughly: 6oz cups grated cheese; 3oz finely ground ham; 1 can condensed tomato soup, 1 tsp. prepared mustard, 1 tsp. grated horse-radish. Spread generous amount of mixture on slices of bread or toast. Grill open sandwiches under broiler until lightly browned. Garnish with parsley.

SPREAD SUGGESTIONS

Put equal parts of Bermuda onion and good Swiss cheese through a meat grinder; spread on buttered bread, cut into small pieces.

Fry bacon crisp, let it dry out, then chop it into fine pieces. Mix with peanut butter and spread on crackers.

Mix chopped ham, hard-boiled egg and mayonnaise for another good spread.

Mix red or black caviar with cottage cheese and a dash of garlic.

Mix chopped lobster and crab-meat with mayonnaise and anchovy paste.

Spread on unsalted crackers.

STURGEON SLICES

Dust very thin slices of smoked sturgeon (or smoked salmon) with white pepper, then decorate with a few chopped chives.

TOASTED CRAB MEAT

Take fresh or canned crab meat and mix with chilli sauce, celery salt and a little pimento. Spread on crackers or toast strips, or put mixture in pastry shells (they come from bakers or in boxes from the grocer) and bake under the grill for a few minutes.

TOMATO CANAPÉS

Cut 3 large tomatoes in half. Cut 6 rounds of bread, and toast. Spread upper side with thin layer of anchovy paste mixed with creamed butter, then with thin layer of mayonnaise. Place tomato halves on each. Dust with salt and pepper and cover tomatoes with thick layer of whipped cream to which 2 table-spoons of well-drained horse-radish and a little grated onion have been added. Dust with paprika and grated carrots.

Caviar

FROM STURGEON
WHO SELDOM NEED URGING

Since the spawn of the Volga sturgeon is best with no other flavour to disguise its own peculiarly sweet and pungent, slightly salty and pleasantly fishy perfume, the real gourmet takes his caviar 'neat' spread on extremely thin buttered black bread ('tartine', to the French). Others squeeze lemon juice over the fish-eggs, spread the caviar on thick slices of hard-boiled egg or even on wedges of cheese, or sprinkle the crumbled yolks of hard-boiled eggs across the top of a caviar 'sandwich'.

If caviar in any form reminds you of your childhood's cod liver oil, it may be that you haven't tasted the good, 'real thing', considered the greatest delicacy in the world of edibles. Only the sturgeon yields real caviar: the so-called 'red caviar' is merely salmon eggs, and a processed caviar which comes from catfish, whitefish, shad or mullet has been artificially dyed. But even among the real caviars there is a confusing variety – so here's a translation of the words you see on caviar cans:

Beluga – large grains

Ossiotra – grains from a sturgeon weighing not more than 700 pounds

Sevruga – from a fish about 200 pounds

Sterlet – from the smallest sturgeon – the tiniest eggs

0 – black caviar

00 – medium black

000 – fine grey

FRESH CAVIAR

Whole eggs. Fish ovaries are cleaned of all fatty matter, the membranes are skilfully removed, the eggs are strained through seven sieves before being put into seasoning brine then into kegs, then into cans.

PRESSED CAVIAR

Made from either premature ova, or from eggs damaged on the sieves. Because pressed caviar is less attractive, the eggs being broken, it is much cheaper than fresh. But it is less salty, more tasty and considered to have a more interesting consistency.

Soups

DUCK-SOUP WAYS
TO BUILD A REPUTATION

When the automatic can opener crowded out the fine art of soup-making in most homes, cagey male cooks realised that the field was wide open to them. Not only did they yearn for un-standardised soups of character themselves – soul-warming soups of appetising bouquet and myriad ingredients – but in the disappearance of the beauteous bowl they saw the ideal starting point for their own kitchen-pleasing. These days, all you have to do is make soup at home and you're labelled a cook. Make a good soup, a distinctive soup, a soup your friends can rely upon, and you're a chef.

Here are countless soups from which to choose your speciality: thick onion soup to forestall hangovers and restore good fellowship after a hard night's pub-crawling...rich bouillabaisse...aristocratic vichyssoise...companionable chowders. Here are soups to serve as meals in themselves, soups to pave the palate for entrees to come, soups to tuck away in the refrigerator for sudden hunger. Here, too, are suggestions for lifting canned soups from the expected to the taste-treat. So take your time and take your choice. And when you find *The* Soup with which to anchor your culinary reputation, when you add the personal touch with makes it yours, 'you, too, can be a soup-er man!'

CANNED SOUPS

To give your lazy-man's soup that indefinable 'umpf,' try mixing can with can. For example: a can of bean with bacon soup mixed with a can of condensed pea soup (plus a can of milk); or bisque of tomato with clam soup; chicken soup with cream of mushroom; mock turtle soup with pea; chicken with celery soup; cream of oyster and tomato, diluted with milk and seasoned with paprika and sherry; chicken gumbo with vegetable, dashed with Worcestershire; onion soup with chicken gumbo; pepper pot with chicken noodle.

Look out for the unusual varieties of soup – cheese soup, for example, or haddock chowder – as well as for the best brands of the classic favourites. In solo or combination all canned soups are the better for imaginative seasoning, too. Try sherry, bitters, mustard, Worcestershire, chopped chives, lemon slices wherever they seem appropriate – and sometimes where they don't.

BRAZILIAN CONSOMMÉ

Take 4 cups of canned consommé, a quarter pint of whipped cream, 1/2 tsp paprika, 2oz finely chopped brazil nuts. Heat soup, put cream on top of each cup and sprinkle with paprika and finely chopped brazil nuts. Or open a can of creamed pea soup, add a dash of onion, 1/4 tsp nutmeg and sprinkle with brazil nuts.

CRABMEAT À LA NEWBURG SOUP

You can go very sophisticated on this with a minimum of effort. 1 can cream of mushroom soup, 1 can asparagus soup, 1 cup milk, 1/4 pint cream, 1 can crabmeat and 3 tablespoons sherry.

NOT CANNED BUT MANNED SOUPS

ALE SOUP

Try this one on your next stag gathering. 1 quart of ale, juice of 1/2 lemon, dash of lemon peel, 1 stick cinnamon, 1 tbsp. potato flour, salt and sugar to taste. Put ale in saucepan with lemon juice, cinnamon and seasoning to taste. Stir continuously, and when hot add the potato flour diluted with a little of the hot soup. Stir and serve.

BEER SOUP

One bottle of beer...when hot add a pint of hot milk in which yolks of 2 eggs have been stirred plus salt and sugar to taste. Serve with fried bread. Or slice or grate some black bread (pumpernickel) into dark beer, with sugar, lemon peel, a sherry glassful or Kummel liqueur, and a small piece of ginger. Let it come to a boil, then strain. When ready to serve, add a lump of butter and salt according to taste.

BOUILLABAISSE

While there are many women cooks who can prepare a fairly presentable bouillabaisse the dish reaches the heights only in the hands of a man. And for every lover of the dish there is another recipe, in fact there are as many bouillabaisse schools as there are for juleps. This recipe permits variation and exceptions.

Begin with a white fish, haddock is preferred, allowing one pound for each guest. Remove the head, tail, fins and backbone and place them in a quart of water and boil until the eyes fall out of the head. Strain the juice and you have a soup stock. Replace the stock in the pan and add:

One clove of crushed garlic

Two sliced onions

One cup of olive oil

One cup of white wine (Chablis, Rhine or Moselle)

One green pepper chopped

One teaspoon saffron

Salt and pepper to taste.

If you have any or all of the following they may be added:

One dozen oysters with liquid

One dozen clams with liquid

One cup of lobster, crab meat or shrimps (fresh only)

Start your liquid cooking and add the vegetables and the fish and later the shellfish. Let it simmer twenty minutes stirring slowly so that the fish does not break up, and serve on top of coarse toast.

CANJA SOUP

(A Brazilian Speciality)

Salt and pepper a fat hen, and let it stand for half an hour. Meanwhile slowly fry a sliced onion in fat; add a minced garlic clove and go on frying until the onion is a golden brown. Add the jointed chicken, and let it fry under close cover until lightly browned on one side, then turn it and fry the same way on other side. Wash half a cup of rice thoroughly, and after draining it add to the chicken together with a quarter of a pound diced ham. Cover the pan and continue the slow frying process but shake occasionally to prevent sticking. Add two quarts of boiling water and one bayleaf, some parsley, and a sprig of marjoram. Simmer until the chicken is tender, then take it out and remove all bones, cut the meat into pieces and return it to the soup.

CARAWAY SEED SOUP

(The most healthful soup on record, according to Joseph Knoepffler of the Passy Restaurant in New York.)

Brown a tablespoonful of flour in a little lard or butter, stirring it constantly so it won't burn. Add a teaspoonful of caraway seeds (for four helpings). When the seeds being to crackle – in about a minute – pour a pint of cold water over them. Cook for ten to fifteen minutes, add salt and pepper, strain, and serve with croutons.

CLAM CHOWDER

20 clams
1 slice fat salt pork
1 onion, sliced
4 potatoes, diced
1 cup fish stock
2 cups scalded milk
1 teaspoon salt
2 tablespoons butter
1 tablespoon Worcestershire Sauce
4 pilot biscuits

Wash the clams and throw into a hot, closed pan for a few seconds to give up their own liquor. Then remove clams and strain juice through cheesecloth. Cut pork into cubes and fry to melt out the fat. Cook onions in pork fat five minutes, then strain the fat into the soup pan. Parboil the potatoes in 1/2 pt water and add water and potatoes to fat. Cover and simmer ten minutes. Add fish stock and clams. Add hot milk, salt, butter and Worcestershire Sauce. Split pilot biscuits, soak in a little cold milk and add to the chowder. And also, for Sunday morning – add two teaspoons of Worcestershire. Serves 4.

CONSOMMÉ À LA ROYAL

Bring to boiling point two quarts of good stock; remove it from the heat and add a tablespoonful of beef extract, one quart of scalded milk, salt and cayenne to taste. Mix well, and add two teaspoonfuls of onion juice; place where it will keep warm, but not boil. For garnishing beat the yolks of two eggs until light, add a 1/4 pint of stock, mix; add a dash of white pepper, and a grating of nutmeg, pour 1/2 in deep into a small pie tin; stand this in a shallow pan of hot water; place in a moderate oven to harden; do not allow to brown. When firm, cut into diamond-shaped pieces; put them into the consommé and serve. Serves 12.

COLD CREAM OF CHICKEN INDIENNE
(From Amando's, New York)

4 chopped onions, 2 stalks celery, 2 bayleaves all smothered in butter with 1 tbsp curry powder and 6 tbsp white flour. Add 2pts canned chicken broth and 1pt milk. Put mixture in your refrigerator for 2 or 3 days (this is the secret of its success) before serving. Serves 8.

CREOLE GUMBO
(From the Roosevelt Hotel, New Orleans)

Stay home some week-end and get to work on: 1oz butter, 3oz lean, raw, dice ham, 1 small white onion and 1 green onion, a leek, a green pepper and a stalk of celery, a clove of garlic and a dash of parsley, a shallot, a clove and a dash of paprika; then a few ounces of cut okra, 12oz raw shrimps, peeled, 1 cup crab meat, 1 small can tomatoes, 1 quart of stock, salt, pepper and bouquet garni.

The secret of the whole thing is in the 1/4 tsp of gumbo filé – a powder made by the Indians of the Louisiana bayous from the roots of the sassafras tree. The New Orleans Import Company is the concern which keeps it on file, so to speak. It is occasionally available in specialist shops, but otherwise you can make do without.

Here's the way you put the stuff

together. Fry the ham, white and green onions, leek, green peppers and celery in butter, add shrimps and crabs and fry until all liquid has been rendered and nearly dried; add dry shallot, garlic, parsley and fry a little longer, then add paprika and tomatoes. Add the bouquet garni, consisting of clove, celery, bay leaves and thyme all tied together. Season to taste and let cook for 20 minutes. Last few minutes add the gumbo filé, being very careful not to let the soup boil while adding the filé or afterwards. Serve with dry sherry. Serves 6.

CUCUMBER SOUP

Makes 2pts cream sauce, add 3 cucumbers peeled and sliced thinly. Cook slowly until soft and transparent, then rub through a sieve. Reheat, season with salt and pepper, add ¼ pt cream and 2 tsps. of bitters. Serves 5.

ONION SOUP

Stay-uppers in Paris have known for years of the curative properties of onion soup and have trundled themselves down to the markets for a bowl alongside the truckmen. This is not the Paris onion soup but comes from Burgundy, and is made according to the old Tisseyre formula.

Take about five pounds of onions. Peel and slice them thin. Put in an iron pot or French cooking dish. Add six bouillon cubes (or better yet, a cup of soup stock or a can of beef broth), then take a loaf of French bread, break into small pieces and put in the pot. Cover this with enough water to submerge the ingredients. Put a lid on the pot, let it come almost to a boil, and then push to the back of the stove to simmer all day. Just before you are ready to serve, add one pint of thick cream. The bread by this time is dissolved, and the soup has the consistency of purée. Serves 6.

OYSTER STEW

Plunge freshly opened, plump oysters (at least 6 per person) into a pan of rich cream. Add gobs of unsalted butter and heat over low flame until the oysters' edges crinkle into smiles. Never let the cream boil. Serve with great crunchy seafaring biscuits. For a variation, toss in a handful of live oyster crabs to give it sea spice.

POTAGE 'BILLY BY'

Take a quart and half-fresh mussels, wash them. Place in a pan with two chopped onions, a little parsley and some freshly ground pepper. Add a bottle of good dry white wine and put on a high heat for fifteen minutes.

In a deep bowl beat eight egg yolks with a good pint of thick cream and a generous piece of unsalted butter. Add to this the strained liquid in which the mussels cooked. Now remove the mussels from their shells and mash the meat firmly, adding this to the rest. Cook on a low heat, constantly stirring with a wooden spoon. When the concoction begins to stick to the spoon just before boiling, strain once more through a cloth, throw in another piece of butter, season to taste, and serve very hot. Serves 4.

POTAGE SANTÉ

Melt one and a half tablespoons of butter or fat in a casserole, and add a chopped onion. Cook for five minutes. Add a palmful of sorrel, and cook for another five minutes. Throw in two large potatoes diced small, salt, 2½ pts of hot water, and cook for forty-five minutes. When cooked, strain. Take the yolks of two eggs, mix well with a small amount of milk or cream, add to this a little of the soup, mix well again, and add it to the soup. Correct seasoning and serve with fried croutons. Serves 4.

POTATO SOUP WITH MUSTARD

Peel 3 potatoes; cook with 1 onion and 1 stalk celery in 3 cups boiling water. When tender mash through purée sieve and add 2 cups thin white sauce and 2 tsps. mustard, just before serving. Gives it considerable élan.

PURÉE OF TOMATOES

(From The Players, Hollywood)
Dice a strip of bacon, half a carrot, half an onion, and a bayleaf, and fry all this in a little butter. Cut into pieces eight tomatoes and add to the concoction together with a little sugar, two ounces of rice and two cups of consommé. Simmer until all the ingredients are soft. Rub through a sieve, add some consommé and a lump of butter just before serving and just after you garnish the soup with peeled, diced tomatoes fried for a minute in butter.

SEMOLINA SOUP

Brown a tablespoonful of semolina or hominy grits, per person in a little lard or butter, stirring the all the while with a spatula. Pour a ½ pt of water per person over it, and season to taste. Cook for five or six minutes, and serve. You may cook a few vegetables in a different vessel, adding them to the semolina soup.

VICHYSSOISE

This is especially recommended for the warm months. Set 6 sliced leeks, 1 small sliced onion, 2 medium-sized sliced potatoes, 2 spoonfuls of butter, pepper and salt to taste, in a covered saucepan. Place over a slow fire in order to cook slowly until the whole is reduced to the consistency of a paste. (Be sure not to brown.) When ready, put through a sieve, add one quart of chicken or beef consommé; mix well and allow to cook off. Then add 1 cup of sour cream; again mix and place in the refrigerator. When serving, sprinkle lightly with chopped chives. Serves 6.

WATERCRESS SOUP

1 small bunch watercress, 3 cups water, ½ small onion, 1 tsp salt, ¼ tsp pepper, 4 tsp butter, 3 tbsp flour, 3 chicken bouillon cubes, ½ pt cream, croutons. Wash and chop watercress. Add to water and onion, which has been sliced, add salt and pepper. Boil slowly for ten minutes. Remove the heat and rub through coarse sieve. Melt butter and add flour, add bouillon cubes to soup, then add to butter and flour. Add cream and serve with croutons. Serves 4.

Fish

TIPPING THE SCALES IN EPICURE'S FAVOUR

Dangle bait like this before your guests, and they'll bite – with delight. After suffering steam-table tastelessness or misplaced housewifely economy, any palate will perk up at the taste of fresh fish, properly prepared – by a man. Women don't seem to understand fish – and, we suppose, vice versa. Call upon your fishing-trip memories to guide you in selecting only the freshest fish at the market. Gills should be bright red; fish should sink, not float, in water. Then hook on to the suggestions, plain and fancy, below. You won't have to fish for culinary compliments once you've served these sea beauties:

BAKED FISH

A satisfactory way to prepare any fish is to sprinkle some flour in a buttered pan, so that the fish won't stick. Then place the fish in the pan, together with shallots and parsley chopped fine, and butter on top. Bake for twenty minutes; and a few minutes before it is done, pour a glass of dry white wine and the juice of a half lemon on it. It is against culinary principles to use garlic in cooking fish, except smearing a crouton or two with a clove.

CARP À LA POLONAISE

(Courtesy of the Polish Restaurant in New York)

One 3 lb carp

One lemon

One stalk of celery

One onion

Two lumps of sugar

Six seeds of black pepper

One pinch of ginger

1pt beer

1pt water

2oz. gingerbread

1 1/2 oz butter

1tsp of prune jam

1oz raisins

1oz currants

1oz almonds

1oz nuts

1 glassful of red wine

Clean the carp well and cut into pieces one and a half inches thick. Slice the celery, the rind of lemon, chop one onion, put in a skillet with 1pt water and boil. When the celery is soft, squeeze in some lemon juice and place the carp in the mixture. Boil for twenty minutes, then take out the carp carefully and put it on a plate; keep it warm.

Strain the remaining mixture and put back in the skillet; add the chopped-up gingerbread, beer, butter, prune jam, sugar, raisins, sliced almonds, peeled nuts and other ingredients and boil. Pour this mixture over the carp, and some of the remaining sauce may be served separately. Serves 6.

COURT-BOUILLON

Although it is most important in the alchemy of fish cookery, few people know the secrets of a good court-bouillon. It is the united cooking of fish, water, wine, vegetables, and seasoning. But the vegetables must be put on about an hour before the fish, otherwise they won't get done and their perfume will not infuse the fish; in other words, the fish must cook in the vegetable water that already is so good that it could be eaten as is. Then before you put the fish in, envelop it securely in a thin piece of linen or some other kind of thin, clean rag. If you don't do this, the fish might fall into little pieces. Don't ever cook fish too long; it isn't meat. If you want to retain all the flavour and perfume of the fish, do not cook it over a high heat, just simmer. The liquid of the court-bouillon is used for soups and sauces, or if strained, it can be put away in bottles if all of it is not needed immediately. The fish is eaten hot with a sauce and vegetables, and what remains is eaten another time, cold, with a sauce that complements cold fish.

Here are several ways to make court-bouillon:

1 Simmer together two quarts of water, a pint of milk, a generous quantity of salt, and the juice of a half lemon. Place the fish in this after about twenty minutes and simmer till tender.

2 Two quarts of water, salt, vinegar, two carrots sliced in small round shapes, two small onions, a bouquet garni, peppercorns according to taste; cook for a half hour before you add the fish.

3 Two quarts of red or white wine, one quart of water, and all the

other ingredients mentioned in recipe No. 2. (This court-bouillon is very good for making fish sauces.)

4 Two quarts of water, salt, garlic, one carrot, one branch of celery, one onion, one clove, a bouquet garni. Cook very slowly for a half-hour. Strain, and add a quart of milk. Now put in your fish and simmer, don't bring to boil. (This kind is excellent for soups.)

And here's what to do with leftover liquid:

COURT-BOUILLON SOUP

Place your court-bouillon – minus the fish, of course, for you've eaten that – in a pot together with an equal amount of water. Add diced potatoes, sliced carrots, leeks, watercress and a bit of sweet cicely. Cook till vegetables are tender; add a glass of white wine and season with salt and pepper. Finally, add a small piece of butter and pour it over small pieces of toast in the tureen.

CRAB MEAT RAVIGOTE

Mix the fresh crab meat with cold Ravigote sauce, made the following way: Add finely chopped chives, tarragon, chervil and parsley to a half cup of mayonnaise. Stir in a little spinach juice for colouring; add a little garlic and capers.

FILET OF FLOUNDER HOLLANDAISE

Put half of a chopped carrot and a quarter of a small onion in salted water and boil slowly. Wash and dry the fish, salt it and roll and fasten it with the aid of toothpicks; then cook it in the boiling water for ten minutes over a medium flame. While the fish is cooking, make your sauce by melting one and a half tablespoons of butter, stir in a half tablespoonful of flour, one egg yolk mixed with a splash of milk, a few drops of lemon, pepper and salt to taste and four tablespoons of water in which the fish was cooked. Pour the sauce over the fish.

FILET OF SOLE-ANYMAN

Get some filet of sole (real lemon sole is well worth the added cost over flounder). Put it in a pan with some butter, one tablespoon of vinegar, one thinly sliced onion, salt and pepper and a cup of white wine. Cook for ten minutes covered. In the meantime have a half pound of mushrooms sautéed in butter, with perhaps a taste of good oil. After the fish has cooked, pour the mushrooms over it, and more wine, then bake in an oven for another ten or fifteen minutes. You'll probably have to eat this with a spoon.

FILET OF SOLE MARGUERY

Poach the filets in a liquid made from one square of butter, four ounces of white wine and two ounces of water. (If you have a good culinary sense, you don't have to measure.) Coat the filets with a white sauce, and garnish with mussels, mushrooms and shrimps, all of which have been previously cooked. To make the white sauce: Add to the liquid in which the fish was poached two yolks of eggs and some butter. Cook slightly and strain, season to taste. Then add a little whipped cream, and glaze.

FILET OF STRIPED BASS
Bonne Femme

Take flat sauce pan and butter it well. Place in it some chopped shallots and parsley and then lay the fish in the saucepan. Season with salt and pepper and add some sliced mushrooms. Sprinkle some cooking wine sauce and fish broth over the filet of bass. Bake ten minutes. Place the fish on the serving dish and pour over it the sauce of the cooking pan after it has been thickened with the yolks of three eggs and a little butter. Serve very hot.

FISH IN DARK BEER

3 pounds of fish (carp, pike or bass)

1 tablespoon vinegar

2 chopped large onions

4 tbsp of butter

2 tbsp of flour

2 tbsp of brown sugar

5 peppers (whole)

2 ground cloves

1 tspn Worcestershire sauce

1 pt dark beer

Clean and scale fish, cut in three-inch slices. Brown onion in butter, add flour and cook for three minutes. Add beer and all other ingredients except the vinegar. Boil this sauce to the thickness of thin cream and put fish slices into it, and continue boiling till the fish is well done. Finally add vinegar and continue boiling for another two minutes. Pour sauce through strainer and serve separately.

FISH MAYONNAISE
(Excellent for leftover fish)

Use any cooked fish. De-bone and cut in pieces. Make a mayonnaise, and cover thinly the bottom of a dish with it. Place a layer of fish on this, and cover the fish layer with mayonnaise, and so on until the fish is used up or the dish is full. Place the dish for two hours in the refrigerator. Chop some sweet pickles, olives, capers and a little tarragon and mix well. Add this to a cupful of mayonnaise, which you saved, mix well and pour over your fish. Serve cold.

FISH RAGOUT
(Matelote)

You can make this dish with one species of fish or several. Best combination is haddock, cod and eel. Cut the fish in about three inch squarish pieces; remove the skin. Put a few pieces of diced bacon in a pot, together with chopped parsley, small onions, salt and pepper, a glass of white wine, a glass of water and your fish, and bring to a boil. After this, put in a moderate oven for 20-25 minutes. Take out the fish, place on a dish and keep warm. Add a glass of good red wine to the liquid, bring to the boil, add a piece of butter mixed with a little flour to thicken. Correct the seasoning, pour sauce over the fish and serve.

CANNED LOBSTER
À LA NEWBURG

Heat two teaspoonfuls of butter in a pan. Add to this three tablespoonfuls of flour, and mix it with the butter with a wooden spoon. Take care that it does not burn. Add a pint of hot milk and, stirring constantly, mix it thoroughly with the flour; otherwise it will get lumpy. Cook and stir for fifteen minutes over a low flame.

Open a can of lobster, and dice it. Heat one teaspoonful of butter in another pan; add the lobster, salt and pepper it, and add a bit of paprika. When you see it is getting hot, pour in a wine glassful of sherry. Now pour the sauce you have prepared over the diced lobster, but not too much of it – just enough to cover it. (If you have some sauce left over, you may use it the next few days, for this cream sauce keeps, and goes with most entrees.) Cook over low flame for ten minutes. If the sauce seems too thick, add a bit of milk. Add some cream a few minutes before serving.

LOBSTER ESCALOPES
Cook the lobster in a court-bouillon. When it cools in the liquid, remove the tail, cut in escalope sizes and plunge the slices into hot butter in a pan. Take the rest of the lobster meat, break it up into little pieces, pass through a sieve, add to this hot tomato sauce, a small glass of brandy or whisky, heat and mix and pour this sauce over the lobster escalopes.

LOBSTER XAVIER
Boil your lobster and, after it has cooled, split lengthwise in two. Remove the shell remains intact; dry the shell. Dice the meat and put the small pieces in hot butter. Add a little cream to it and a cup of Mornay sauce, prepared the following way:

Beat the yolks of two eggs together with a cup of Béchamel sauce (melt 3 tablespoonfuls of butter, add to this 3 tablespoonfuls of flour, cook till golden brown, add gradually 2 cups of milk, stir constantly and add a slice or two of onion. Cook for one hour over low flame and strain through fine sieve), add a tablespoonful of butter, and a little grated cheese.

Mix the diced lobster meat with the Mornay sauce, fill the shell with the preparation and cover the top with more Mornay sauce. Sprinkle with grated cheese and brown in a hot oven.

OYSTER SNACK
Sauté finely chopped celery in a little butter and when it is tender add one wineglass of sherry (for each dozen oysters) and stir until very hot. Into this drop your oysters (six for each guest), and let them cook until their little edges start curling. Then arrange six oysters for each guest on a piece of toast and pour the liquid over them and serve, preferably with a glass of sherry.

BROILED OYSTERS
Drain the oysters and lay them on a napkin to dry. Pepper and salt them, and broil them on an oyster broiler (if you have one) or a small gridiron. The oysters must not smoke, and they must be cooked quickly. Put a bit of butter on them just before serving.

DEVILLED OYSTERS

1 pint oysters

1 tbsp butter

3 shallots

1/2 pt cream

Salt

Nutmeg

Cayenne

Mustard

Worcestershire Sauce

Mushrooms, chopped

Parsley

Egg yolk

Buttered cracker crumbs

Wash and chop oysters, cook shallots in butter for 3 minutes, add flour and stir until well blended, then add milk and cream. Bring to boiling point and add oysters and remaining ingredients except yolk and crumbs. Simmer for 12 minutes. Add egg yolk, put mixture in deep halves of oyster shells, cover with buttered crumbs, bake for 15 minutes in a medium oven.

OYSTERS MORNAY

Bake oysters on the half shell for four minutes. Remove from oven, cover them with sauce Mornay and bake until brown. To make sauce Mornay, boil one pint Béchamel sauce (see Lobster Xavier recipe) with one-quarter pint of oyster liquor. Reduce by a good quarter and add four tablespoons of Gruyère and 4 tablespoons grated Parmesan cheese. Put the sauce on the fire again for a few minutes and ensure the melting of the cheese by stirring with a small whisk. Finish the sauce away from the heat with four tablespoons of butter added one by one.

OYSTERS RAREBIT

Bring one cup of oysters to the boiling point and save the liquor. Melt two tablespoons of butter, add 4 ounces of fresh cheese, but in small pieces; 1/4 teaspoon of salt and a sprinkle of cayenne. When the cheese has melted, add the oyster liquor and two eggs slightly beaten. When smooth, add the oysters and serve at once on toast.

OYSTERS À LA ROCKFELLER

Bake oysters on the half shell for four minutes. Remove from oven and cover the oysters with very fine chopped spinach and onion, bread crumbs, cheese and a few dashes of Herbesaint. Bake until brown and serve.

SHRIMPS IN BEER

4 cups beer

3 shallots

2 onions, sliced

5 tbsp. butter

2 pounds raw shrimps

Sprig of parsley

Bayleaf

Celery

5 tablespoons flour

Cook the beer with the onions, shallots, bayleaf, parsley and celery, for about 15 minutes; add peeled shrimps to the broth and cook for another 15 minutes; season with salt and pepper. Remove the parsley bouquet and bind the sauce with the butter and flour which have been creamed together. Serves 6.

Steak

VARIATIONS ON A FAVOURITE THEME

Ah, steak – plain, unadulterated beef – is paradise. You no doubt have your favourite method of preparing the queen-beef: perhaps you sizzle it briefly beneath a hot broiler flame to produce a cut-with-a-fork, uniform tenderness; or maybe you throw it into a smoking skillet to form a crusty surface encasing the steak's juices. But if ever you should tire of the wondrous pleasure to be found in such unadorned beefsteak, get into the speciality-sweepstakes with these variations.

BACHELORS' BEEF STEAK

1 thick Porterhouse steak
Olive oil
Salt
Pepper
2 cups beer
4 tablespoons butter
2 tablespoons flour
1 pound fresh button
  mushrooms

Marinade steak in oil, season on both sides and broil to desired doneness. A few minutes before the steak is done, fry mushrooms in butter, season with salt and pepper; add flour, then steak juice from broiler pan and beer. Stir well while cooking. Let come to a boil, then pour over steak and serve.

MAC NAMARA BEEFSTEAK

This is ideal for picnics, but can be emulated at home. For a starter, try spring onions, radishes and celery. For dessert, the indicated titbit is a baby lamb chop broiled over the charcoal. It may sound silly – but try it!

Procure from a good butcher a steak at least three inches thick. Have it cut from the choicest part of the cow and take nothing inferior. When ready for the food part of the picnic, take the steak and cover both sides with pepper and salt. Then completely encase the steak in a coating of wet coarse salt to the thickness of a quarter inch. Next place some white paper napkins on top of this, to keep the salt in place. Prepare a fire of wood or charcoal in a pit edged with stones. Place the steak in a heavy wire grill and cook for about ten minutes on each side.

Now knock off the outer layer of salt, which comes off in one piece. Then slice the Porterhouse and sirloin down in thin strips. Throw these in a pan of butter, which you have set on the fire. Serve the slices of meat on a half slice of bread, which has been dipped in the butter.

SURPRISE STEAK

Choose your favourite cut, which should be free of bone. A thick rump, if you can find a tender one, is ideal. Lightly dust each side with salt, them apply a thin film of prepared English mustard – English, because that is the fieriest variety. Next – and here you are going to be scandalized, as I was when the editor told me, and before I had tried it out – cover both sides of the steak as thickly as it will stick on, with powdered sugar. Sound terrible, doesn't it? But wait! Burning sugar produces an intense heat. Ask any visiting fireman who has fought a conflagration in a sugar refinery.

Broil your steak about three minutes on each side. The sugar will first melt, then harden into a blackened shell that hermetically seals the pores of the steak, preventing the loss of a crop of juice, or a whiff of flavour. Crack and peel off the sugar shell, and carve, the 'blood following the knife'. Contrary to your fears, the steak will not taste sugary. The intense heat will have absorbed all the sugar into its protective shell, and at the same time have charred the surface of the steak beautifully.

PLANKING

Take a large plank, as large as will fit comfortably in your oven. It should be of non-resinous and well-dried wood – birch and maple are the best – and the top side scooped out to the depth of half an inch. If this is too much trouble you may be able to purchase an already prepared plank at the hardware store. Place the plank in the oven and let it get hot enough for butter to melt immediately. Place your meat with the best side up in the centre. About it lay the vegetables that are to accompany the main piece, then replace them all in the oven. Do not worry about the smoke; it's all a part of the flavour.

Stew

HOW TO DO RIGHT
BY A MAN'S DISH

Second only to steak in its standing as a Man's Dish, stew surpasses most entrees. Accompanied by a bottle of wine and a green salad, followed by a cup of strong coffee and perhaps a hunk of cheese – who could ask for more?

Some stews may indeed by 'only' stews – thin, watery, with microscopic amounts of meat. But not these samples below, and not the stews you 'invent' when you're familiar with the two basic types:

The White Stew Family, includes all stews made of lamb, veal, fowl or hare, sautéed with onions, bacon or butter and salt and pepper; sometimes potatoes are cooked in these stews, and occasionally thickening is added. The liquid is usually a light stock (or water), or a white wine.

The Brown Stew Family, consisting of stews made of beef, usually cooked with carrots, turnips, onions, peas and other vegetables, and herbs and salt and pepper. Red wine is more often used than white; the stock is usually bouillon – although, of course, water may be used for both types.

Here are samples of each. Take it from here!

[39]

BOEUF BOURGUIGNON

Get two pounds of lean beef for four people. Dice the meat. Make a pickle out of a magnum bottle of red Bordeaux wine, small onions, carrots, celery, garlic, thyme, one bayleaf, three cloves, parsley. Marinade meat in this pickle overnight. Then take out the meat (sorry, you can't use the pickle for anything else afterward), sprinkle the meat cubes with a dash of brandy or whisky, salt and pepper them, and sauté them in a pan with finely diced bacon and some flour over a brisk heat for ten minutes. Then pour in a new bottle of red wine, adding mushrooms and small onions. Cook for about two hours over a very low heat. Don't open the lid, and don't forget that a stew boiled is a stew spoiled!

IRISH STEW

Wash and drain two pounds of mutton, removing the skin, gristle, and excess fat. Cut meat in square pieces. Put them into the pan with one pound of already peeled and quartered potatoes and two onions. Add seasoning and water or stock, remembering that the liquid must cover no more than half the food. Stew slowly. Add another pound of potatoes one hour before serving; these will cook gently, and will not lose shape like those put in earlier. Serve hot, with the whole potatoes around the edge, meat in the middle, and the gravy poured over.

OXTAIL STEW WITH BURGUNDY

Cut two oxtails into small sections. Brown them in butter. Add carrots, celery, onions, mushrooms, pota-toes, a bayleaf, salt and pepper and 2 glasses red wine and cook until the meat is done, about three hours. Thicken with 2 tablespoons butter browned with 2 tablespoons flour, juice 1/2 lemon and parsley. (Beurre Meuniere.) Serves 6.

HUNGARIAN PORKOLT

Get one and a half pounds of shoul-der of veal, dice it, chop up two large onions, brown them in a pan with a tablespoonful of lard on a very brisk fire – do not burn – and add a half lump of sugar. Put the meat in the pan, and turn down the flame. After fifteen minutes add one tablespoonful of paprika, one tomato, one green pepper cut up, salt to taste. Let it simmer for one hour. Do not open the lid! Do not add any water or liquid! Serve with boiled rice or boiled potatoes. Serves 4.

This same porkolt (which, in rough translation, simply means singed) may be made with suckling pig, pork, mutton, fowl, duck, turkey and goose.

(**Note**: In the goulash category there are three specific branches: goulash, a soup dish with beef and potatoes in it; the above described porkolt, which is a paprika dish without cream; and finally paprikasch, which has sour or sweet cream in it. There are several important points to remember in making goulash or its relatives; one is not to brown the onions too much. It is also better to use lard than butter. All goulashes feel hap-pier with half a lump of sugar in them.

Game

COOKING THE KILL

Game can be cooked in a spick-and-span tiled kitchen, of course, and even by some women (who usually are good shots as well); but a log cabin or an open grill is the logical place – and a man is the proper cook. For the nimble Nimrod, who would tame his game to the table as well as he tracked and shot it, Esquire offers these pointers:

No furred animal or feathered fowl should ever be fried.

Small game of any sort is best broiled or roasted except rabbits and squirrels which are strewed like larger game, geese, big ducks and venison, or made into 'salamis' and pies. Any game reheated for hash is fine, but it must never be recooked, only warmed up.

In broiling, a strip of salt pork or thick bacon should always be tied tightly over the breast for automatic basting.

Birds, be they tiny teal or tremendous wild turkey, must always be plucked dry. Scalding them kills the flavour; and equally in cleaning the carcass no water should ever touch the insides. Wipe with a towel dampened in spirits, vinegar or wine, depending upon personal taste.

How 'high' game should be or whether the tail of small birds should be eaten is also a private matter, yet it is true that long hanging improves the flavour, giving that gamey taste. So no duck should be cleaned too soon and a rabbit shouldn't be opened short of three days.

Citrus fruits go best with birds, and tart jellies with furred game. Corn on the cob, as stuffing for quail, or in the luscious form of green corn oysters, is as perfectly suited to all wild flesh as it was when it accompanied the first barbecued hump of buffalo.

Serving diced croutons fried in butter with a wild biddy may seem but an effete, inconsequential detail. But, as a matter of fact, it's the essence of the whole matter; the juices of game are the very life blood of the dish and not one drop can be sacrificed. So serve crunchy toasts and browned crusts always, all sorts and varieties of sippets and soppets, rusks, fried breads and flaky vol-au-vents, any kind of crisp dunking bit to sop up the salubrious sauces. Especially is this true with the smaller birds.

Every bit of reed birds, snipe and woodcock are indeed so precious that only the feathers and whistle are discarded. The fact is, their toothsome little bodies are never even opened, but cooked and eaten whole. And those in the know esteem the brains as the most delicate morsel.

BEAR

To be specific: Here's how to handle your next bear. Hack off his paws, skin them and set them to soak in a salty, winey marinade for two or three days. Then stew with ham trimmings and tasty vegetables for seven or eight hours. Cool them, dry them, slice lengthwise in four parts, add pepper and cayenne, roll in melted lard and bread crumbs and broil for half an hour. Serve with redcurrant jelly – and who's afraid of the big black bear!

DUCK

You may not feel up to stewing one wild duck in the pressed blood and raw juices of its mate, as they do down in New Orleans where wooden duck presses are as necessary sporting equipment as cork decoys. So instead, stuff one with sage, onion, bread crumbs, butter, salt and pepper; and roast its mate without either seasoning or dressing. This makes a palatable contrast when a little of each bird goes on every plate. But a great way to do a duck is Hunters' Style – *Salmi de Canards Sauvages A La Chasseur* as

the menu-makers say. Just clean and wipe a brace of birds, cut off the legs, wings and breast and set them aside out of reach of the cat while you lightly salt the carcasses and giblets, bake them about the length of time it takes to smoke a cigarette and then hash all together, put even the bones into a stewpan, pour in a couple of glasses of beef or veal broth, add a snugly tied herb bouquet and set to simmering for fifteen minutes or so. In a separate saucepan melt a ball of butter about the size of a tame duck's egg, lightly season the legs, wings and breasts and brown them for a few minutes on each side. Squeeze over them the juice of a lemon and toss in the whole rind, grated. Then put in a cupful of strongly flavoured meat broth and strain in all the gravy from the cooked carcass and giblet hash. Simmer for fifteen minutes and serve surrounded by diced butter-fried croutons. A big bowl of sliced oranges makes a swell side dish.

MIXED GRILL

Grill or roast cutlets, breasts, filets, titbits and giblets of anything you have in the bag; rabbit, quail, venison, squirrels, or anything except hell-diver and prairie dog. Meanwhile, toss up a panful of bacon and French fries. Saw a hearty round off a handy hardwood stump, heat it, pile up the murphies and bacon in the centre, lay the 'scorched' meat all around, remember fingers were made before forks, and have some gherkins, a head of celery, salt and pepper hard by to pep up the feast. And drink with it whatever you don't get enough of at home.

POSSUM

This is a real favourite in the southern states of the USA. In true hillbilly style boil it tender in well salted water right in the iron camp kettle. Lift the boiled possum right into the baking pan and go get yourself a bundle of green sassafras twigs. Tweak off the tip ends to toothpick size and stick them an inch deep into the meat and so thickly you can tell a tenderfoot it's porcupine. Use butter and a little water in the bottom of the pan so it won't burn while baking. Sprinkle well with pepper and dot with butter. Boil sweet potatoes, peel, lay them around the possum and let them finish baking with him. Munch corn bread with the feast to bring out the full sassafras flavour, and it's good enough to make you lick all ten fingers.

PRAIRIE CHICKEN

Yank off the big breasts of dark meat and broil them, with butter for basting. They must be hand-picked of course, wiped clean, never washed and, like all grouse, quail and small birds, dipped in melted butter before they're ready for the fire. A hash can be made of the leftovers, legs, giblets, etc., moistened with claret and lemon and a dozen stoned olives stirred in at the finish. Served with diced croutons fried in butter this speciality of the wheat states is tasty enough to make a prairie pioneer turn on his spit.

RABBIT

There are more than hundred standard recipes for cooking the ubiquitous rabbit – each as tasty as the next. Rather than give you so many succulent styles as to get in your hare, Esquire tips you towards rabbits roasted with oysters:

Chop a dozen oysters with a good-sized sponge cake to make the stuffing for Brer Rabbit. Add butter and a mere soupcon of cayenne. Roast the stuffed rabbit an hour, eat him in 10 minutes with a sauce of the oyster liquor and butter simmered together with a little flour for thickening, more cayenne and a touch of cinnamon.

Then there's this treatment for the rabbit, by a French Canadian guide:

Recipe of the Rabbit to the Wine White or the Wine Red

Some slices of salt pork, some butter, some onions, a little oil, and put to fry the all in a pot. Cut then the rabbit into small pieces and put with the rest. When that is a-frying add one of two spoonfuls of flour and well rouse (stir) the whole. Next add one quart of the Wine

White or the Wine Red, some parsley and a leaf of bay, some salt and pepper. Make it to cook on a fire very slowly. Empty it on a plate hot and then it eats fine.

SQUIRREL PIE

Even folks who never go hunting with anything more deadly than a Kodak should know how to make a squirrel pie. It's easy once they're skinned, cleaned; and all the hairs and stray ants wiped off with a wet cloth. Save the blood, for the blood of squirrels and rabbits is as precious as those last drops of any game gravy caught by the croutons. To keep the blood from curdling pour a little vinegar or lemon juice into it. Use the heart, liver and kidneys too. Cut the rest up in joints. Mix a pound of finely chopped beef suet with a pound and a half of flour, lots of salt and plenty of pepper. Mix a pound of finely chopped beef suet with a pound and a half of flour, lots of salt and plenty of pepper. Stir in cold water to make a pie crust dough. Then butter an earthenware dish and line it with the dough, almost an inch thick. Lay in the meat and giblets, pour the blood over and enough water to fill the pie-dish half way. More salt and pepper, much more. Then put a dough cover over all, wet the edges and make them stick tight so no bubbling drop of gravy can get out, but leave a little safety valve in the middle for the steam. Bake about two hours in a moderate oven. When the top crust is yellow-brown put on buttered paper to protect its complexion. Take it to the table in the dish that made it.

VENISON

Deer is best when shot in autumn after fattening on autumn berries. And of course it should be young, but even if it's old, it is still the quickest cooking flesh there is. You roast a haunch the same as you do beef; only not so long and moistened with a whole cup of water. Garnish with watercress and serve with redcurrant jelly or, better still, wild grape. Ten minutes to the pound is the rule, although a doe cooks faster than a buck.

A venison steak is cooked to perfection when covered thickly with damp salt. Broil it, then crack off the crust of salt and you've really got something. But most folks choose the saddle, which must be well larded before roasting. Steaks and cutlets are fine for broiling and the rougher parts are stewed with mushrooms, herbs and cloves of garlic.

Sauce

TOPPING TOPPERS

Dr Johnson defined sauce as simply: 'Something eaten with food to improve its taste'. What's sauce for the goose is not always sauce for the gander, however. That's why the following recipes for a few excellent sauces include suggestion for their most sauce-picious use.

There are only two basic sauces know to culinary art: brown sauce and white sauce, or in professional parlance, Espagnole and Allemande. The basis of brown sauce is a good stock that may be very easily made of left-over meats or gravy. An excellent stock can be made of some raw bones baked in a hot oven until brown and then cooked in water with onions and carrots and garlic for a couple of hours. If you have this stock you need only to add your various ingredients in order to get a certain definite side sauce. All brown sauces keep well in the refrigerator, differing from white sauces.

The bases of white sauces are milk, cream, butter or white stock, from a chicken carcass or feet of fowl, thrown away necks and even heads of fowl, veal bones or inexpensive cuts of veal. But if you want to make a sauce for fish, use as a base some of the liquid in which your fish cooks.

BECHAMEL

Named after the maitre d'hotel of Louis XIV of France, this the father of all white sauces and is exceedingly simple to prepare. Melt two tablespoonfuls of butter in a saucepan, adding to it two tablespoonfuls of flour, mixing well and cooking until a nice brown. Add a cup of boiling milk gradually, stirring constantly and add a small onion as well. Season to taste and cook for 15 minutes over a very low heat. Strain and serve.

BROWN SAUCE

The recipes below can be varied to make any number of lesser sauces. melt two tablespoonfuls of butter in a saucepan and brown two carrots and two onions in it, whole or sliced if you like. Mix two tablespoonfuls of flour in it and cook until a nice brown. Add a good pint of stock, a bayleaf, thyme, tomatoes, peppercorns, garlic, celery, parsley and simmer for one hour. Season to taste, Strain thoroughly and add 1/4 cup of red wine or sherry, and cook a little longer before serving.

HOLLANDAISE SAUCE

Divide 4 ounces of butter into 3 pieces. Place one piece in top of a double boiler with 2 egg yolks and 2 teaspoons lemon juice. Cook, stirring constantly over hot, but not boiling, water. Gradually adding the remaining butter. Cook continuing to stir for about 2 minutes or until it is as thick as desired.

Remove from the heat and add ¼ teaspoon of salt and a few grains of cayenne. Continue heating for a few minutes. Add, if desired, 3 tablespoons of cream.

MARCHAND DE VIN SAUCE
(Excellent with steaks)
Cook 2 finely chopped shallots in a generous glass of claret until the liquid is reduced by half, then add 2 tablespoonfuls of butter, salt and pepper to taste and finely chopped parsley.

MAYONNAISE
This thick sauce, so good with fish, hard boiled eggs, veal, cold chicken and vegetables, calls for efficiency and undivided attention.

Mix the yolk of 1 raw egg with a little dry mustard, salt and pepper with a spatula. Add a tablespoon of lemon juice and mix. Now add very slowly, drop by drop, and beating all the time a cupful of olive oil. Add another tablespoon of lemon juice. Beat well.

PARSLEY SAUCE
Chop up some parsley very fine – the more parsley the better the sauce. Add a little lemon juice or vinegar and salt and pepper. Also add a little chopped onion or garlic to taste. Saturate this will salad oil, mix thoroughly and pour over your dish. goes very well with cold boiled fish, boiled meats or boiled potatoes. Makes royal fare out of last night's leftovers.

WHITE WINE SAUCE
Reduce white wine and vinegar of the same proportions to two thirds by cooking. Add a glass of red wine and a finely chopped shallot, also some pepper and a bit of thyme an bayleaf, crushed. Add a large spoonful of veal stock. Let it boil for a few minutes, taste it and adjust the seasoning. pass it through a fine sieve and finish it up by adding a little finely chopped parsley.

SAUCE FOR BOILED FISH
Melt 8 ounces of butter and mix in with it four hard boiled eggs, chopped very fine. Season with salt and pepper.

Salads

TOSSED UP, NOT FLOSSED-UP

Old French dictionaries said that salads are a *'réunion de choses confusément assemblées.'* The trouble with this definition, that salads are 'a union of things confusedly assembled', is that hostesses and tea-rooms take the definition too seriously – they marry pineapple to cream cheese, nuts to marshmallow, mayonnaise to onions, and so on. Women go berserk when it comes to salads; they try so hard to be unique that in their zeal they really confuse things.

A purist in gastronomy acclaims only one category of salads: green leaves. For instance, lettuce, romaine, chicory, dandelion or whichever happens to be in season, should be well washed and dried, seasoned with salt, pepper, oil, vinegar and mustard. It was about such salads Brillat-Savarin said that they 'refresh, invigorate, comfort, and it is my habit to say that they even rejuvenate.' In these uncomplicated but marvellous salads the most important thing is that the leaves should be fresh, crisp and vivid in colour, the pepper freshly ground, the salt preferably sea salt, the oil real olive oil, the vinegar wine vinegar and mustard in powder form.

The proportions are a matter of taste, although here, too, there are some established rules as, for instance, that the measure should be one spoonful of vinegar to two of oil. And first the salt must be dissolved in the vinegar, then the mustard powder, then the oil added, and finally the pepper. Observing this order is important, for the salt and the mustard do not easily dissolve in the oil. If you like garlic, smear a small piece of dry bread (for the heel of the loaf) with it, and mix it in with the leaves. And if you have some herbs, a sprinkle of tarragon, chives, or chervil helps after having tossed and turned the salad forty times.

But there are other formulae as, for instance, this advice from an 18th century cleric:

> *Two large potatoes pass'd through kitchen sieve*
> *Smoothness and softness to the salad give;*
> *Of mordent mustard add a single spoon;*
> *Distrust the condiment that bites too soon;*
> *But deem it not, thou man of herbs, a fault,*
> *To add a double quantity of salt;*
> *Four times the spoon with oil of Lucca crown,*
> *And twice with wine vinegar procured for 'town';*
> *True flavour needs it, and your poet begs,*
> *The pounded yellow of two well-boiled eggs.*
> *Let onion's atoms lurk within the bowl,*
> *And, scarce suspected, animate the whole;*

And, lastly, in the flavour'd compound toss
A magic spoonful of anchovy sauce.
Oh! Great and glorious, and herbaceous treat,
Oh! T'would tempt the dying anchorite to eat,
Back to the world he'd turn his weary soul,
And plunge his fingers in the salad bowl.

BEER CABBAGE SLAW

1 medium sized head of cabbage
1 green pepper, shredded
2 tblsp celery seed
1 tsp salt
1 tsp minced onion
1 cup mayonnaise
1/4 pt beer
1/4 tsp pepper

Shred cabbage. Add green pepper, celery seed, onion and seasoning. Thin mayonnaise with beer. Add to cabbage. Toss thoroughly. Chill. Serves 6 to 8.

CRANBERRY CASHEW SALAD

Cook 8 ounces cranberries with 1/2 pint water and 4 ounces sugar. When they pop, add 1 1/2 table-spoons unflavoured gelatine which has been soaked in 1/4 pint cold water, to the hot mixture. Mix well. Throw in 2 ounces ground, salted cashew nuts, one chopped apple, 3 sticks diced celery. Turn into moulds and chill. Serve on lettuce. Serves 6.

FINGER SALAD

Wash a head of romaine, and dry each leaf separately and well with a napkin. Toast a piece of bread, stroke it gently with garlic, cut the toast into small squares and place them in a salad bowl; put the leaves of romaine over the toast. Soft-boil two eggs, and spread them over the leaves. Add three tablespoonfuls of olive oil, lemon instead of vinegar, salt, pepper, a bit of Worcestershire sauce, mix very well, and finally sprinkle grated Parmesan cheese on top. This is the only salad that may properly be eaten with the fingers.

MUSHROOM SALAD

Mix in equal proportions, canned mushrooms sliced into strips, cold cooked potatoes cut into rounds, and strips of raw celery. Season with salt, pepper, olive oil and wine vinegar.

POTATO SALAD-BEER DRESSING

6 medium sized potatoes
1 tblsp vinegar
2 tblsp olive oil
1 tsp salt
1/2 tsp pepper
1 tblsp finely chopped onion
3 sticks finely diced celery
1 Lettuce

Dressing

1/2 pt milk
1 tblsp butter
1 1/2 tblsp corn flour
3 tblsp cold water
2 tsp dry mustard
1 tsp salt
Dash of cayenne
1/4 pt cold beer

Cook potatoes in rapidly boiling salted water until tender. Drain and peel. Cut into small cubes. Make a marinade of next six ingredients. Turn over warm potatoes and let stand until thoroughly cooled. Heap in lettuce cups. Heat milk with butter. Mix corn flour to a paste with cold water. Add to milk with seasonings. Cook over hot water, stirring constantly until thick. Cool. Add beer slowly, beating until smooth. Force through a sieve if necessary. Serve on potato salad. Serves 4.

SALADE MELANGEE

Rub salad bowl with a cut clove of garlic. Then cut the following into chunks and slices and drop into the bowl: lettuce, cucumber, radishes, tomatoes, celery, carrots, watercress, chicory. Then mash 4 ounces cream cheese with 2 tablespoons cream. Add and mix in 1½ tablespoons anchovy paste, 1 tablespoon caviar (optional) and one half cup French dressing. Mix thoroughly, then pour this dressing over the salad. Toss and serve.

THOUSAND ISLAND DRESSING

Mix together very well two tablespoons of chilli sauce, one cup of mayonnaise, a half teaspoonful of Worcestershire sauce, the same amount of chopped chives and chopped pimentos.

Desserts

SWEET FINALES

A bit of fruit and cheese, a cup of coffee, perhaps a little brandy – that's just desserts for the finest meal. But even so, as your sweet tooth tells you, there'll be times when you'll want to serve something more elaborate. Here are your best bets, ranging from homely to elegant but carefully skirting the trite territory of ice-cream and cake.

The fact that it does not appear among these dessert recipes is not to indicate that a good deep-dish apple pie floating with syrup and shot full of cinnamon, is not a proper topping for your favourite dinner – even if it *should* be served on a hot-water bag and garnished with digestive tablets. Rather, the pie's absence is due to the exhaustive (and exhausting) instructions for piemaking to be found in any ladies' cookbook. Besides, as George Ade wrote in Esquire many years ago, 'Pies develop character as well as heartburn. Pie eaters are rugged characters. When they make up their minds to anything their opinions cannot be altered, not even by the use of bicarbonate of soda.'

APPLE DITLER

Quarter and core four eating apples. Boil in a 1/4 pint of water and 2 ounces sugar to which add the grated rind and juice of half lemon. When apples are tender remove to a plate, then add two glasses of good white wine. Cook for ten minutes more and serve the apples with the hot sauce poured over the fruit.

APPLE TODDY

Roast 6 apples that have been covered with molasses, butter, brown sugar and cinnamon. Add water to cover bottom of pan and after they are tender, pour brandy over. Should be piping hot before serving.

BABA AU RHUM

Cool 1/4 pint scalded milk to lukewarm. Add 1 cake compressed yeast, crumbed, 2 ounces flour and 2 tablespoons sugar. Stir until smooth. Cover and let rise in a warm place for about 1 hour. Cream 2 ounces butter, gradually adding 6 tablespoons sugar. Beat until light. Add 1/2 teaspoon salt, 2 teaspoons grated lemon rind, 3 eggs, well beaten, 6 ounces flour and yeast mixture. Beat well, about 15 minutes. Half fill small moulds, which are well buttered both on the bottom and on the sides. Cover, and let rise until doubled in bulk, about 1 hour. Cook 40 minutes in a moderate oven (350 degrees).
Syrup for the Baba: boil 2 ounces sugar and 1/4 pint water together for 5 minutes. Cook and add a double shot of rum. Pour syrup over Babas, and let soak in. When ready to serve, add some apricot jam on the top of the Babas.

BAKED ALASKA

On a board place a layer of spongecake; lay on vanilla ice cream. On top place a dry, well-beaten mixture of four egg whites and 2 ounces icing sugar. Brown in hot oven for a moment and serve immediately.

BAKED GRAPEFRUIT, HAWAIIAN

Slice the fruit in half and score. Drop spoonfuls of pure molasses between the slices and in the centre. Sprinkle with cinnamon and bake under broiler for 5 minutes.

CAFÉ ROYALE

Take a cup of hot coffee, black, without sugar. Place a lump of sugar on the spoon across the top of the cup and then pour a shot of bourbon across the sugar into the cup. Touch a match to the sugar and when it has burned out, drink the coffee.

CANTALOUPE OBOLENSKY

Make a round incision about 3 inches in diameter at the stalk of a cantaloupe, take out the plug, and remove the seeds with a spoon through the hole in the melon. Then pour 2 wineglasses of sherry into the melon, replace the plug, and place the melon in cracked ice for an hour. Finally, cut into halves and serve in soup plates.

CRÊPES SUZETTE

First of all make plain French pancakes. Like this: Sift 3 ounces of wheat flour in a bowl and break into this three eggs. Add 2 tbsp melted butter, 1/2 tsp salt; mix it well; pour in 2/3 pint cold milk very gradually, mixing constantly for about five minutes. Gently butter a frying pan and put it on the cooker; when it is hot, pour in batter to make 5-inch cake and after two minutes of cooking, turn it over and bake it on the other side, also, for two minutes. Place the pancakes (you should have about a dozen) on a hot plate and cover them up and prepare your Crêpes Suzette sauce. Melt one ounce unsalted butter in chafing dish over low flame. Add one ounce sugar, 1 tbsp grated orange rind, 1 tsp grated lemon rind, 1/4 pint orange juice. Cook for 3 minutes. Roll pancakes and heat in sauce. Add some brandy, Cointreau, Curaçao and cherry brandy. If you only use one liqueur, Cointreau is best. The mixture, the proportions, the strength of the Crêpes Suzettes sauce is entirely up to you. Set aflame, and serve at once on warm plates. Serves 6. This dish is not difficult, but it does require some care.

FUDGE

Melt 5 tbsp of butter in a saucepan, add 1/2 pint of milk or cream, 1 1/2 pounds of sugar, 5 ounces chocolate and stir gently until chocolate melts. Boil without stirring to 236 degrees F, or until a teaspoonful forms a soft ball when dropped in cold water. Allow to cool, add vanilla flavour or chopped nuts, and beat with a wooden spoon until it begins to stiffen. Pour into buttered pan to three-quarters of an inch thickness; mark into squares at once.

GRAPE MOUSSE

Soften 2 tablespoons granulated gelatine in a small amount of grape juice. Heat one pint grape juice to simmering, and add gelatine mixture. Mix well; let cool. When it starts to thicken, beat well and fold in 4 egg whites, beaten until stiff. Serve in sherbet glasses, garnished with lady fingers.

Two cups heavy cream, whipped, may be used instead of the egg whites, in which case the mixture should be frozen before serving. Serves 8.

KIRSCH BANANAS À LA PETE

A quickie dessert can be made in three minutes by slicing some bananas lengthwise and cooking for a few seconds in butter. Then sprinkle with sugar, add Kirsch or brandy, light and let burn for a few minutes, then serve.

THE POOR KNIGHTS OF WINDSOR

Cut some slices of bread about half an inch thick; soak the slices for a while in white wine and sugar. Beat two or three yolks of eggs. Take the bread out of the wine and dip it in the egg yolks. Heat a little butter in a pan; put in the bread and fry brown. Place the bread slices on a dish and sprinkle cinnamon and sugar over them. Drink a glass or two of white wine with it.

PREACHERS' DELIGHT

Legend has it that a Methodist parson, partaking of a synod banquet in a nearby Babylon, was noted to be pushing watermelon seeds into his Bible. The mystery turned on the dessert: a fine ripe watermelon into which had been poured one quart of good old Bourbon. The minister had hoped to plant such seeds in his garden.

Try it this summer, putting the melon in the icebox overnight.

RED WINE FRUIT JELLY

2 tbsp sparkling powdered gelatine

1 pint Red Wine (Burgundy type)

4 tbsp granulated sugar

1 tsp lemon juice

3 sliced peaches – or other fresh fruit

Soften gelatine in 1/4 pint water until dissolved. Bring Red Wine and sugar to heat; not boil, over a low heat. Add gelatine and lemon juice. Stir well and pour half the mixture in cup glasses – half full. Add the fruit and put in icebox to chill. When firm enough fill the cups with the rest of the jelly so fruit will not float on top. Serve with sweetened whipped cream. Serves 6.

RICE PUDDING WITH APPLES

Cook 2 ounces of rice in a quart of milk. Stir an ounce of butter until nearly liquid, with 2 ounces of granulated sugar, four yolks of eggs; mix this with the cooled milky rice, and add to this the egg whites which you have beaten to a froth. Pour half of this mixture into a vessel that has been smeared with butter lightly on the bottom, placing on top six peeled apple halves from which cores have been removed and in their stead apricot jam introduced, together with a half lump of sugar soaked in rum. Pour the remaining half of the rice mixture on top and bake in a moderately

hot oven for forty-five minutes to one hour. Serves 6.

RUM ICE CREAM

Beat 5 egg yolks, and add 2 ounces sugar, 1/8 tsp salt and 1/2 pint warm milk. Cook over hot water, stirring until thick. Let cool; add 1/2 pint heavy cream and 3 tbsp rum. Freeze in ice cream freezer.

SABAYON SAUCE

Mix 3 tbsp of sugar and four egg yolks in a mixing bowl, and beat very hard. Add a wine glass of Marsala or sherry and the juice of half an orange; cook over hot water, beating constantly, until thick. Serve with sponge cake. Serves 2.

ZABAGLIONE

Beat 6 egg yolks, then add 1 teaspoon of vanilla extract or 1 vanilla stick, 6 tablespoons of granulated sugar and place in a double boiler. Increase the heat gradually and beat constantly until it thickens. Pour into glasses and serve warm or chilled if preferred.

If desired cold: Let get cold and then place in refrigerator; decorate with pistachios. If in a bowl, place lady-fingers around the bowl, and sprinkle with wine, then pour the zabaglione into it and decorate. Serves 4.

Note: This is darned hard to make and takes much patience and slow cooking – which is probably one of the reasons it's so expensive in restaurants.

Cheese

HIGH 'C' OF THE MEAL

'Dessert without cheese is like a pretty girl with only one eye,' wrote Brillat-Savarin, French gourmet of the 18th and 19th centuries. A high 'C' of the meal, cheese is not only gifted as a topper-offer and tumtum tranquillizer, but also as an amplifier of the accompanying wine. Professional wine-tasters, in fact, use cheese to sharpen their keenness; it coaxes shy wine subtleties out into the open.

As to which species of cheese is greatest, opinions are so personal and so controversial, that the only way to avoid bad blood is the Assortment System: serve a platter, of cartwheel format, so your guests may choose their favourites. Here are some of the most popular cheeses:

Mould-mottled *Roquefort* gets its impetuousness from outwardly placid sheep's milk. But it doesn't come direct from ewe to you: there's an elaborate business of interpolating specially treated breadcrumbs, followed by pro-tracted curing in cold, naturally drafty caves and grottos.

Italy's *Gorgonzola*, similarly mottled but made of cow's milk, is larger, crumblier, and even less timid. After a salad whose dresser didn't spare the garlic this cheese can be faced and exterminated with surprising facility. On the blander side there's creamy, discus-shaped *Bel Paese* – soft and self-controlled.

Tricky to deal with are those sob-sisters-under-their-skins, *Camembert*, *Brie* (larger), and *Pont l'Eveque* (square), hailing from regions west and east of Paris. Yet it's a case of the weepier the better. The cheese code of honour stipulates that, before sacrifice, they be given their due chance to mellow on the pantry shelf (refrigerator is too cold) till ready to swoon at touch.

Authentic *Switzerland Cheese*, tattooed with the name, gets its delectable ping from the milk of special cows that in summer pasture high up near the edelweiss. The holes are mementoes of natural carbon dioxide gas, sponta-neously generated as in champagne.

Low pastures have their good points too, the Dutch insist – backing the claim with cannonball *Edams* and fishcake-shaped *Goudas*.

England's flaky, golden *Cheshire* and purple-veined *Stilton* are nice work if you can get them. And if you can get Stilton-in-Port – ummm! America's patented creations include *Liederkranz*, buddy of beer.

For crunching and conveying, split and toasted Bent's swaddled in a nap-kin, are the traditional. Or try any of the various crackers from the crispies bearing their own butter to the everyday and evergood 'soda cracker'.

Coffee

THE CUP THAT CHEERS

When coffee was introduced to Europe in the 16th century, people thought that it rendered women frigid and even barren. A law was promptly passed in Constantinople giving husbands the right to prevent the use of coffee by their wives. Maybe that's why the average woman, to this day, can't make a good cup of coffee. It must be that, basically, coffee is a man's drink. When subjected to the economies of drugstore waitresses or the casual inattention of wives, the cup that cheers but does not inebriate is apt to become a mean, thin liquid with almost unlimited capacities for discouraging real coffee lovers.

So know ye this: no aspect of your cooking skill will bring you greater or more lasting pleasure than the ability to prepare the drink that stimulates wit and digestion. Coffee splices all loose ends, greets the cheese gladly, and spreads a mantle of aromatic warmth.

Here are some of the basic rules for making it properly:

1. Use only freshly roasted, freshly ground coffee.
2. Start with cold, fresh water – and if it is to be poured over the coffee when boiling be sure to pour it as soon as it boils, lest the oxygen be dispelled and the water be made tasteless by long boiling.
3. Make sure your equipment is spotlessly clean.
4. Always measure ingredients carefully and time the brewing period exactly – so you can be sure to duplicate your method time after time once you have settled on the proper combination of water, coffee and time.

Beyond that, your own taste is boss. Using one of the following systems, experiment until you've reached coffee of the proper strength to match your memory of the best cup of coffee you ever sipped. The proportion usually recommended is 1 tablespoon of coffee to each cup of water, with an extra tablespoon of coffee 'for the pot'. With men who ken coffee, 2 tablespoons to 1 cup is a more favoured strength. And some, to avoid long perking or simmering and the consequent bitter taste, use even a greater proportion of coffee. But there's as much variation in the strength of different coffee blends, as there is the tastes of coffee-drinkers, so suit yourself.

GLASSMAKER COFFEE

Water is put into the lower bowl, upper bowl is fitted in, complete with filter or rod, then coffee is place in the upper bowl. When water is hot, it rises through the tube into the upper bowl. Then as soon as steam comes up through the tube and agitates the mixture, the heat is turned off. Gradually, then, the coffee filters into the lower bowl – from which you serve it. Or you may prefer to allow the coffee to simmer in the upper bowl for 2 to 5 minutes, for a stronger brew. Or you may put only an inch or so of water in the lower bowl (enough to create a vacuum when it boils) and heat the remainder of the required water separately, to be poured over the coffee grounds as for drip coffee. In any case, pulverised coffee is used.

OLD FASHIONED COFFEE POT

For this method, favoured of our forbears, coffee should be coarsely ground. Dry coffee goes into the pot (or ordinary saucepan) first, then cold water. Bring to a boil, simmer for 5-8 minutes, then take it off the stove. A dash of cold water will settle the grounds – or an eggshell thrown into the brew at the outset will have the same effect. Even so, you need a strainer for pouring.

PERCOLATOR COFFEE

Use the same proportions as for pot coffee, but use medium-ground coffee – half-way between drip grind and pot grind. Coffee goes into the basket in the percolator, water into the pot; then the water 'perks' through the coffee until it is the strength you like: about 8 minutes. With a glass percolator, you can see how you're doing throughout the process; others have a glass piece on top so you can get a glimpse of the brew as it perks.

Whatever the method used, coffee is best when freshly made. Once you've got your own coffee making timed, you'll know just when to fade from your dinner table in order to have fresh coffee ready by desserttime or maybe you'll latch onto an electric coffeemaker that can do its fragrant work right at the table. Ben Jonson said, 'As he brews, so shall he drink'. Good drinking!

Midnight Snacks

CURES FOR BOOZE
IN THE NIGHT

The man who can ask his friends in after the theatre or other late functions, not just to raid the icebox or 'have a drink,' is a man who is going somewhere – to his cupboard and his chafing dish, of course, but also to the top of his friends' hit parade. Develop your snack-knack with:

CHEESE FONDUE

Heat 1 cup of White Wine in an earthen chafing dish rubbed with garlic. Then add, stirring with a fork, 1 pound of methodically hacked-up Swiss openwork cheese, alias Emmenthaler.

On the side, mix 1 tablespoon of flour in 3 tablespoonfuls of Kirsch. Add this to the main show, which is still cooking and must still be stirred.

Hunklets of crusty French-type bread about the size of lemon quarters, now come into play: one of these brod micken, impaled on a fork, is used as a stirrer until sopped with Fondue; then seized lightly with the teeth as though it were a toasted marshmallow. But what a morsel! Whereupon the other player takes over, pronto, because if stirring were allowed to lapse, even briefly things would get stringy. With one participant working while the other eats, the alternation is kept up, punctuated by as many sips of Kirsch as can be crowded in, until no more Fondue is discoverable.

No wine or beer should be partaken of with a Fondue, as either, even at room temperature, would chill it into ropiness inside its consumers. Afterwards, coffee with Kirsch puts a seal of safety on the situation, and from then on one may eat or drink anything with serenity of assimilation. First and last, Fondue is Kirsch's private dish.

OYSTERS AND CELERY FROM
BILLY THE OYSTERMAN

Chop some celery and sauté in butter and, when tender, add to this the oysters (two dozen to three sticks of celery) with their liquor, and simmer until the edges of the oysters curl. Add a glass of white wine on the sweet side, season and serve in its own sauce.

WAFFLES

Equipped with a waffle iron, a package of biscuit or pancake mix and a lubricated imagination, you're a cinch for a successful snack session. Here are a few variations on the standard-but-still-good waffles and syrup routine:

Cheese waffles: sprinkle grated cheese atop our regular waffle mixture.

Ham waffles: sprinkle 2 ounces diced, uncooked ham over the batter before closing the iron. Especially good with scrambled eggs.

Pecan waffles: sprinkle an ounce of broken nut kernels over batter before closing iron. Good with brown sugar as a change from syrup.

Chocolate waffles (for the ladies): add a couple of squares of melted chocolate to your standard mixture. Serve with ice cream or whipped cream.

Corn waffles: use prepared corn-muffin mix on your waffle iron, and you'll have waffles fit for the Old South, sho nuff.

Or, for *really* different waffles:

WELSH RABBIT (1)

Place 1 tablespoon butter and 1/2 pint ale or beer (which may be stale) in a chafin dish or double boiler. When warm, put in 1 pound chopped or grated Cheddar cheese and melt unhurriedly, stirring the while, until smooth. Then add 2 egg yolks, which have been intermingled with 1/4 pint milk, dash of salt, and 2 teaspoons Worcestershire sauce. Stir these newcomers into the cheese-scape a moment or two, until thickened.

Serve upon slices of bread whose downsides have been toasted. Sprinkle with paprika. Side issues: celery, olives, salted nuts. Serves 6.

WELSH RABBIT (2)

Cut one-half pound of store cheese into small pieces and place them in the top of a double boiler. Pour over the cheese a 1/4 pint of beer, a pinch of cayenne with a stick or wooden spoon and serve on pieces of toast. Now bring out your bottled beer. Serves 4.

RAREBIT WITH BEER

1 pound cheddar cheese

1/2 pint lager

1 egg

Dash of cayenne

1 tbsp English mustard

1/2 tsp Worcestershire

Salt

2 tbsp of butter

Melt butter in chafing dish or thick frying pan. Grate cheese, add, and melt very slowly. Mix seasonings in a cup with a tablespoon of beer; add egg and beat together. As the cheese melts add the beer, a little at a time, stopping when the mixture has the consistency of thick cream. Stir constantly in the same direction. The melting and stirring in of the beer should take at least half an hour. Be careful that it never bubbles. When perfectly smooth, stir in the egg. The cheese mixture should be hot enough so that the egg thickens it slightly. Pour over toasted crackers or slices of thin toast on very hot plates. Serves 6.

Picnic Supper

AN EASY BUFFET MENU

Particularly in the early stages of your cookery experiments, you might do well to plan something simple and deliberately devoid of the delicate touches. A picnic sort of meal on your terrace is an easy way to entertain large groups without fuss. Baked ham and beans form a popular menu for just such occasions. Add a big green salad, gobs of French and/or brown bread, plenty of beer or red wine and you can count on a successful evening.

BAKED BEANS

1lb pea beans

8oz pound salt pork

1/8 tsp celery salt

1 tbsp brown sugar

1/2 tbsp dry mustard

1 clove garlic

2 tbsp molasses

1/2 pt tomato juice

1/2 tsp Worcestershire Sauce

1 large onion

Pinch cayenne pepper

1/2 pt beer

Pick over the beans, cover with cold water and soak for 24 hours. Drain, cover with fresh water, heat slowly, keeping water below the boiling point at all times. Cook until the skins begin to burst. Test by taking a few beans on a spoon and blowing on them – if sufficiently cooked, the skins will burst. Scald and scrape pork. Put one strip in the bottom of the pot with onion. Add the beans. Mash the garlic clove and mix with the brown sugar, molasses, mustard, Worcestershire, celery salt and cayenne pepper; add the tomato juice and pour over the beans. Top the pot with the remaining salt pork. Cover the bean pot and bake for 8 hours at 275F. When the beans have been baking for 4 hours, add the beer. Uncover for the last hour of baking, so that the rind may become brown and crisp. Serves 6.

HAM IN BEER

18-pound ham
Cloves
2oz brown sugar
1 tbsp dry mustard
2 tbsp vinegar
2 glasses of beer

Cover ham with cold water. Bring slowly to a boiling point. Simmer for three hours. Remove from water. Skin. Score fat in diamond shapes, and stud with cloves. Make a paste of brown sugar, mustard and vinegar. Pour over ham. Bake in moderate oven (350 degrees F) 1½ hours, basting frequently with beer. *Approximate yield:* 24 portions. The juice of the basting on the ham can be made into a delicious sauce to be served on the ham when sliced.

(*Variation:* Put garlic in the water when boiling ham. Bake surrounded by apples, cored but not peeled, the centre of each filled with currants. Baste with wine instead of beer.)

Eat Alone and Like It

JUST PLAIN FOOD

You wouldn't set them before a dainty damsel you hoped to impress, but these homely foods may hit the spot when you're alone and in a shirtsleeve mood...or when your bowling team admits a yen for simple, beersy food. They won't set any gourmets on fire, these hamburger-frankfurter-type dishes, but maybe they'll brighten the corner where you are catching a solo dinner.

HAMBURGER SANDWICH

8oz ground raw beef

1 tsp salt

2 tbsp minced onion

Butter or drippings

1 tbsp Worcestershire sauce

Mix the beef with the salt, onion and Worcestershire sauce. Make into thin cakes and brown on both sides in a hot frying pan containing drippings or melted butter. Turn often, sprinkling with salt each time. When cooked, place between slices of buttered bread or toast and serve very hot.

CORNED BEEF HASH

Mix two parts chopped meat with one part chopped boiled potatoes and a little chopped onions if wanted. Salt carefully, less in the case of corned beef. Add a little pepper. Cook it in a frying pan with butter until well browned, and roll as you do an omelette. Decorate with a poached egg on top, and serve very hot.

MEAT LOAF

Take three quarters of a pound of ground beef and three quarters of a pound of lean ground pork and mix them well together. Also take a bread roll, soak it in cold water for five minutes, and then squeeze it free of water with your hand. Shred and mix this with the meat. Chop up very finely a small onion, beat an egg (both white and yolk), mix these also with the meat, and season with salt and pepper. Mix once more very thoroughly, fashion into a loaf, and spread the white of an egg over it. Heat a tablespoon of fat in a roaster, slide the meat loaf into it. Bake in a medium oven for about an hour. Peel small potatoes and place them beside the meat in the roaster a half hour before the meat will be ready. Baste occasionally. If you prefer you can serve with mashed potatoes. Serves 4.

SAUSAGES OR FRANKFURTERS

Try Swiss *gendarme* (flat in shape), Italian Mortadella (enormous in circumference), Spanish *estramaduran*, an English Cambridge, a Hungarian salami, a truffled French *saucisson royal* or everyday 'hot dogs'.

Either:

Brown the sausage slightly in butter. Add a glass of white wine, simmer for ten minutes. Now take the franks out and place them on slices of stale bread fried previously in butter. Go on simmering the sauce, add to it a few drops of lemon juice, the yolk of an egg, a little gravy, a little butter, and season to taste. Pour the sauce over the frankfurters.

Or:

Skin the sausages, cut them in half, lengthwise, and place half of them in a buttered pie dish. On top of the sausages lay sliced onions which were slightly browned in butter, slices of raw tomatoes, and season. Lay on top the remaining sausages, cover with consommé (canned), and a thick layer of mashed potatoes. Place butter on top and brown in moderate oven.

CASSEROLE MEAL

4 tbsp chopped onion

4 tbsp cooking oil

1 green pepper finely chopped

12oz leftover meat ground (or ground raw beef)

1 1/2 tsp salt

1/2 pt beer

1/2 tsp pepper

2 eggs

1 can whole kernel corn

3 tomatoes, peeled and sliced

Brown the onion, green pepper and meat in the cooking oil. Add salt and pepper. When cool add beaten eggs. Oil a casserole; arrange above ingredients in layers with half the corn, the meat, the sliced tomatoes, the other half of the corn. Pour the beer over and then cover with the breadcrumbs. Bake at 350 degrees F for 45 minutes. Some grated cheese may be mixed with the crumbs if desired. Serves 6.

SAUSAGES IN WHITE WINE

Put one cup of consommé and one and one-half cups of white wine in an earthenware casserole. Put one carrot and one stalk of celery, finely copped, in the wine; when the wine is hot, place one dozen large pork sausages in the casserole, cover and cook over a slow flame. If cooked too quickly the sausages will burst. The length of time for cooking naturally depends on the size of the sausages, so this must be determined by the cook. Serve the sausages in the casserole to keep them very hot; mashed or creamed potatoes will prove the perfect complement. Serves 6.

BOILED PIGS' FEET

Soak the trotters for 8 hours in water. Drain. Place them in a saucepan with cold water, seasoning, and some raw vegetables. Boil for 5 to 6 hours. Remove and cut each foot in two parts. Wet the surface with a brush dipped in melted butter. Roll in very fine bread crumbs and broil them for 15 to 20 minutes over a moderate fire, preferably a charcoal fire.

Breakfast

RISE AND SHINE

Rassling up your own breakfast between dressing operations is a problem of technique. Eventually you'll get to the point where you can fix coffee, eggs and toast by remote control while you're shaving and showering. That's when the corner drugstore will have lost another customer – for no public eatery can match the quiet comfort of breakfast at home.

Here are some of the standbys to snap you out of your bachelor daze of a week-day morning (and to put you in training for 'breakfast for two' performance some day!). And on the next page you'll fine a real praise-raiser of a Sunday brunch for entertaining.

Toast – Your best bet is an electric toaster that pops the toast up at you when it's done. Lacking that, put bread slices under the grill until brown on both sides. For cinnamon toast, spread with butter and sprinkle with a combination of cinnamon and sugar, then replace under grill to melt the yummy topping.

Coffee – see page 55. Breakfast coffee is sometimes less strong than dinner coffee or demi-taste.

Tea – Swill some boiling water around in an earthenware pot, to heat it, then dump out the water. Then into the pot put one teaspoonful black tea for each cup of tea wanted. Bring fresh cold water to the boiling point, pour over the tea, then cover and allow tea to 'steep' about three minutes, or until it reaches the desired strength.

BOILED EGGS

Place eggs in saucepan of boiling water; simmer three minutes. Serve in an egg-cup – English fashion – or dump into a coffee cup in the robust American manner.

POACHED EGGS

Fill a frying pan three-quarters full of boiling water, break and slip eggs in and cook over low heat until the whites are firm and a film forms over the yolks: transfer the eggs with a skimmer to a slice of toast.

SCRAMBLED EGGS

1 tablespoon of milk, 1/2 teaspoonful salt, pepper and 1/2 teaspoonful butter to each egg. Break the eggs into a bowl, add seasonings and milk, beat lightly with a fork. Heat butter in omelette pan, add egg mixture. Do not stir, but, as the eggs cook, scrape gently from bottom of the dish, drawing the cooked mass to one side. Remove from heat when nearly firm throughout and serve quickly.

BAKED SPANISH EGGS

Fry 3 tablespoons chopped onion and 3 tablespoons chopped green pepper in 4 tablespoons butter until slightly brown, then pour into a baking dish. Break 6 eggs into this dish, being careful not to break the yolks. Mix 2 ounces breadcrumbs with 4 ounces grated cheese and sprinkle over the eggs. Cover each egg with 2 tablespoons of beer over the top. Bake in a moderate oven until the eggs are set but not hard. Serve in the baking dish.

OMELETTES

Omelettes are easy to make and easy to spoil. It is really child's play to prepare an omelette – but one false move, and you may as well throw it away. You've got to be on the job every moment it is in preparation; but then, slow and lazy men do not make good cooks anyhow. Crack into a bowl two eggs (for each person) and season them with a pinch of salt and a half pinch of pepper. Beat it unmercifully for five minutes, until the whites and yolks are completely mixed; the more the eggs are beaten, the lighter the omelette will be; and beat it with a silver fork. Do not use fancy kitchen utensils like an egg beater unless you are callous to the contempt of professional chefs.

Take a frying pan and put into it a teaspoonful of best olive oil; do not use butter as it might burn. Heat the oil in the pan until it becomes terribly hot on the brisk flame. When the oil starts to smoke, fume and crackle, pour the eggs into the pan and agitate them gently for no longer than forty to fifty seconds; never dry them out by leaving them longer on the heat, as a dried out or burned omelette is uneatable. Now remove the pan to a somewhat less hot spot on the range and fold the omelette with your fork – the side nearest the handle first – into a half-moon shape. Smear a bit of butter over it; take the handle of the pan in your right hand, a hot plate with a napkin underneath it in your left and with a rapid movement turn the pan right over the centre of the plate. If you have done all this properly you may crow like a cock: 'Ko-ko-ri-ko!' for that is how the French chefs greet a perfect omelette when it is ready. But do not forget that efficiency and quickness count above all, and that an omelette must always be made to order; it is better that the man wait rather than the eggs.

EGGS EN COCOTTE

Slightly warm up individual small earthenware ramekins, and pour in their bottoms a little boiling cream. Gently break the eggs (not more than two in a ramekin) and carefully slide them onto the surface of the cream. Season with salt and pepper, and add a tiny piece of butter. Place the ramekin into a pan of boiling water to reach within half an inch of the brim of the ramekin. Cover (but leave a little opening for the steam to escape), put the pan in the oven for ten minutes, and serve.

Carving

KNIFE WITH FATHER

The fine art of carving was, until recently, as absolutely essential a part of a gentleman's education as a knowledge of horsemanship, swordsmanship, and dancing. In the old days, carving was a rite. With impressive, leisurely dignity, the host set about dismembering the fare, with the result that the first person served was about ready for dessert before the careful carver had lopped off his own meat. These days call for fewer flourishes and more speed.

The first essentials for carving are a good knife and fork. What you want is a knife with a fine steel blade about nine inches long and some depth at the heel: the blade should be slightly curved and should taper to the point. The fork should have large curved prongs, so it will not slip out. A steel and an emery stone are also necessary. The blade can be emeried by laying the heel of the knife across it at about a 30 degree angle, the edge toward you, then draw the knife across the stone toward you lightly without bearing down on it. Reverse and do the same for the other side for about a dozen strokes. This should be done in the pantry. You may use the steel before going to the table but in order to keep the keen edge essential for successful carving, it will be necessary to sharpen the blade during the course of carving. When whetting the blade, the edge should be drawn along the steel towards you, rather than away.

BIRDS

TURKEY AND CHICKEN

First sink the fork at a spot a couple of inches behind the point of the breast bone with one prong on either side of the bone: there is a special place for it, which was apparently designed to accommodate forks and you will find it readily. Now slip the point of the knife under the far wing and make an upward cut for the joint that holds the wing to the turkey, a straight cut well towards the neck so as not to undershoot the joint. If the wing doesn't drop off, get the knife into the joint and break it if necessary. The leg or drumstick and the second joint should be removed in one piece. Make a straight cut for the joint that holds it to the bird. Cut an inch or two above the 'Pope's nose', going as far as you can; then slip the knife behind the joint and cut to the juncture again. This should separate the whole business from the body of the fowl. Once it is off, put the fork

[65]

in the second joint and cut for the juncture of the drum stick and the second joint. Now one side of the bird is stripped of its appendages and you are ready to carve the breast. Put the fork in the same position in which you originally inserted it in the bird, and lay the bird on its side, legless side up, so that the slices of breast, as you carve them, will remain in position until you lift them off. If the bird is left upright, the slices would fall off to the side and, while this is all right with ham and certain other joints, it will not do with turkey: the breast will crumble and the slices be difficult and unappetising to handle. So, lay the bird on the side and cut the slices with firm, even strokes. Slices should not be thick.

DUCK

Young duck or duckling is carved in a similar manner to chicken or turkey. First, the wings are removed and then the breast is either sliced or, if it be a small bird, it is removed in one piece. Next the leg and second joint are removed, divided or served in one piece if it is small.

GOOSE

If you ever have to tackle a roast goose, remember that the breast of a goose, more than that of any other bird, is highly esteemed, and the carver may not have to give much attention to any other part, though some people find the legs excellent.

WILD DUCK, TEAL, ETC.

Epicures consider only the breast of wild fowl worth eating and usually only this is served.

FOWL

Roast and broiled fowl (chickens, capon, etc.) are cut in a manner similar to roast turkey.

PHEASANT

The choicest parts of the pheasant are the breast and the wings, as is true of most fowl. Pheasant is carved exactly as turkey.

PARTRIDGE

There are several ways of carving a partridge. The usual method is to cut the bird along the top of the breast bone and divide it into two equal parts: a half partridge is a fair portion for one person. If it is necessary to make the partridge do for three people, the legs and wings may be easily severed and a leg and a wing will provide a helping, while the breast will provide a third helping. The partridge may also be cut into four equal portions if necessary. Woodcock and pigeon are carved in the same manner – in either two, three or four portions.

GROUSE

Grouse may be carved in the same way as partridge. It is well to know that the backbone of the grouse is highly esteemed by many and considered, along with the same portion of many game birds, to possess the finest flavour.

SNIPE

Snipe are served whole as these tiny birds make but a single helping.

MEAT

Meat should always be cut across the grain, the one exception to this rule being the saddle of mutton which is always carved at tight angles to the rib bones, in slices running parallel with the fibres or grain of the meat. Ham and beef should be cut in very thin slices and lamb, mutton and pork in fairly thick ones.

A round of beef, or ribs rolled, are not so easy to carve as some joints. A thin-bladed knife is recommended. First, cut a thick slice off the outside of the joint at its top, so as to leave the surface smooth, then thin and even slices should be carved.

A calf's head is nearly always boned before serving, and is then cut in slices like any other boned or rolled joint. If it is not boned, you should carve the head in strips from the ear to the nose. With each of these should be serve a piece of what is called the throat sweetbread, cut in semi-circular form from the throat part. (The eye and the flesh around it are favourite morsels with many: they should be given to those guests who are known to be connoisseurs.)

VEAL

Breast of veal consists of two parts: the rib bones and the gristly brisket. These two parts should be separated: then the rib bones may be detached separately and served.

MUTTON

Leg of mutton is comparatively simple to carve. The knife should be carried sharply down to the bone and slices taken from either side, as the guests may desire.

The saddle of mutton is a fine old English dish: it consists of two loins connected by the spinal bone. The meat is generally carved across the ribs in slices running parallel with the backbone and the grain of the meat, and with each portion is usually served a small piece of fat cut from the bottom of the ribs. Plenty of good gravy and red currant jelly should be served with this.

In carving a shoulder of mutton the joint should be raised from the dish and as many slices cut away as can be managed. After this the meat lying on either side of the blade bone should be served by carving it from the knuckle end. The joint can then be turned and slices taken off along its whole length.

PORK

A leg of pork is carved as a leg of mutton: the knife should be carried sharply down to the bone right through to the crackling. A loin of pork, if it is properly prepared at the butcher's, may be divided into neat and even chops and presents no particular carving problems.

HAM

Here the carver must be guided by whether he desires to practice economy of to serve immediately from the best part. Under the first supposition, he will commence at the knuckle and cut thin slices toward the thick part of the ham. If he prefers to serve the finest part first, he will cut across and down to the bone at the centre of the ham.

LAMB

A leg or shoulder of lamb is carved as a leg of shoulder of mutton.

SUCKLING PIG

If you should ever have occasion to carve a suckling pig, don't be alarmed: it is not a very difficult feat. The pig should be served with the head separated from the body, and it is usually sent to the table with the body separated in half. The first point to be attended to is the separation of the shoulder from the carcass. The next step is to remove the leg; then the ribs remain fairly open to the knife. The other half of the pig may be served in the same manner. All parts of a suckling pig make delicious eating but, in serving it, you should consult the preferences of your guests.

FISH

A steel knife and fork should never be used for fish because contact with this metal is apt to spoil its flavour, particularly with certain choice varieties which owe their excellence almost entirely to a delicate characteristic flavour. A silver or plated slicer and fork should be provided for carving and serving fish. Be careful not to break the flakes which ought to be served as entirely as possible, although short grained fish, such as salmon, should be cut length-wise.

LOBSTER

To dress a lobster properly, insert a knife at the centre of the back and cut through towards the tail. Then turn the lobster around and cut through towards the nose. (Be careful to cut towards the tail first, otherwise the shell will most certainly break.) After the lobster is cut, remove the brains. These are usually of a greenish colour and are found at either side of the lobster head. The claw shells should be cracked open with a hammer or nutcracker and are sometimes served as a separate dish.

CRAB

In preparing a crab for consumption, place it on its back and insert your fingers between the shell and the meat. Using your thumbs as levers, push the body away from the shell: then break off the claws, remove the poisonous 'fingers' and cut away the sides of the back shell.

Drink

'There is much to indicate that in our civilisation alcohol has a very useful function to perform and may be a source of increased happiness and decreased hostilities.'
   Karl Menninger

'Let us drink for the replenishment of our strength, not for our sorrow.'
   Cicero

'Here's how!'
   Esquire

Tips on Technique

IT'S THE WAY HOW YOU DO IT

If you would build perfection potables that recondition the human system in three cool sips...if you would cast the spell of friendly hospitality over every gathering, be it planned or spontaneous, around your bar...you'd best capitalise on the years (even centuries) of taste-and-tell experiments made by your predecessors in the world of whistle-whetting.

Here, then, are the open secrets of drink-making:

1. *Use only the best ingredients – and show them proudly, full face, on your bar, not anonymously in suspicious-looking decanters.*
   Selecting 'the best' is a matter for your own taste, but if you can't personally spot a raw whisky or a sad Scotch at first sip, you'll have to trust a reliable dealer, brand-names and indicative price-tags. A drink is, of course, no better than its ingredients – from liquor all the way down to lemon juice. When the budget rears its ugly head, use *your* head: a good blended whisky will do very nicely in mixed drinks, so save that 8-year-old straight bourbon for 'neat' drinks, highballs, and Old Fashioneds. If you're stuck with a cloudy gin and can't bring yourself to break it over the head of the guy who sold it to you, try it in fizzes or Collinses but never in a Martini. If you can't afford a really good cognac, serve a lesser liqueur; use the cheap brandy for a blue flame on the pudding but not for a give-away inhaler.

2. *Use **exact** – not hit-or-miss – measurements*
   If you'd like to vie with the professionals and rely entirely upon your eye,

then spend 48 hours a week manipulating a mixing glass so that it acquires invisible level marks, comparable to the tone spacings that a violinist's fingers deal with on his fiddle strings. Otherwise wield a jigger carefully, not only to arrive at the result intended by the recipe but also to be able to repeat that result again and again.

3. *In mixing, stick to the shake or stir technique prescribed by the recipe.*
   Martinis and Manhattans are stirred in a pitcher of ice, not only to make them icy cold and to blend their ingredients but also to prevent their clouding up as would be the case were they handled in a shaker. Drinks which include sugar, eggs, cream, fruit juice, etc. will be cloudy anyway, so shaking is in order for best mixing. When in doubt, use your noggin: pure liquors are not shaken unless that method is specifically prescribed; seltzer water is never under any circumstances meant to be flattened in a shaker. But when you *do* shake, *shake!* A Ramos Gin Fizz takes the extreme – 12 minutes of shaking – but it follows that any drink which needs a shaker to blend it needs a *good* job of blending (and chilling) done on it.

4. *Use plenty of ice- and wherever possible pour your liquor over ice rather than adding ice to already-poured liquor. Don't use the same ice twice.*
   Except to a Britisher, nothing is more depressing than a warm drink. If you're worried about over-dilution of highballs, use less soda rather than less ice. Ice *cubes* are used for stirred drinks, but creaked ice is the order for shaker-drinks. That makes sense when you think about it, and a bar gadget makes it easy. The main thing is that it be *ice only*, not a pool of ice and water. When crushed ice is called for, as in Juleps and Frozen Daiquiris, you'll pound it in a bag – but, again, make sure it's *dry* before you put it in the glass.

5. *Use prechilled glasses.* When you haven't time to cool them in advance in the refrigerator, fill them with crushed ice and let them shiver while you mix the drinks. Then dump out the ice, *wipe out the glasses* and pour in the drink. That way your cold drink will stay cold, or that ice in the drink won't immediately begin to dribble.

6. *Match your service to your mixing, or attention will be distracted from your good deeds at the bar.* Pour smoothly, cutting off the flow from pitcher or shaker with a sharp uplift or a quick twist to prevent slopping or dripping. Don't fill glasses so full that they spill over at first clutch, provide coasters or cocktail napkins, spear olives or drink-fruit on toothpicks so they can be easily gobbled or removed. Keep the bar clean, and be sure glasses are spotless – and dry. Always recap bottles as soon as you've finished with them.

What the Well-dressed Bar Will Wear

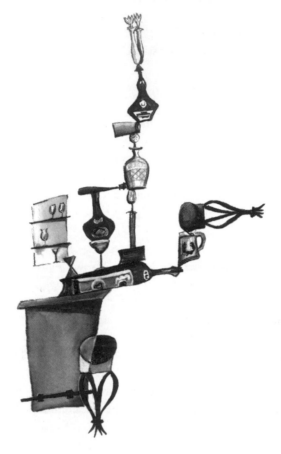

If you were to collect all the bar gadgets on the market, as interesting a hobby as that might be, you'd probably have to build a new wing on your barroom. You'd have a Waring Mixer for frappes, a Hamilton Beach for flips, an electrical unit for hot toddies, a midget refrigerator for ice-cubes and beer and mixes, special racks for wines and, no doubt, a constant hangover. Fun is fun, but so are funds – so here's a basic list of bar accessories.

1 *A jigger measure.* Especially practical is the four-jigger, its quartet of capacities ranging from 3/4 oz. (1/2 jigger) to 1 oz. (a pony) to 1 3/4 oz. (1 jigger; standard cocktail slug) to 2 oz. (enough for a Collins, fizz or generous highball). There are also patented pourers which, installed in bottle necks, dole out precise doses; and some jiggers are built in combination with bar spoons, corkscrews or bottle-openers.
2 *A long bar spoon* – for use both in measuring teaspoons of sugar, etc., and in stirring cocktails.

3   *A muddler-round-based wooden stick* – for mashing sugar and bitters, as in the Old-Fashioned.

4   *A glass or plastic stirring rod*, for use whenever seltzer is involved (carbonated mixtures may collapse at touch of metal).

5   *A bottle opener* (the hook variety)...a beer-can opener...a good corkscrew...a can-opener (in case olives or cherries or the like appear in cans). These often come in combination.

6   *A paring knife* for cutting lemon peels, etc.

7   *An ice pick* and/or a patented ice shaver.

8   *A sturdy bag* and *wooden mallet* for crushing fine ice.

9   *A vacuum ice bucket* – to eliminate frequent trips to the kitchen.

10 *A good cocktail shaker* – or a mixing glass equipped with a screw top and pouring spout. Shaker may be of either metal or glass, but should have a large opening for ice and a small one for pouring. Try to get a non-leak, non-drip variety with removable strainer.

11 *A pitcher* or *tall mixing glass* in which to stir Martinis and Manhattans. See that the container has the handy, moulded lip which holds back the ice while you pour out the drink. If you prefer a mixing glass, you'll need a circular wire strainer to fit over the top for pouring.

12 *Glassware*

    Your glassware repertoire will largely depend on the drinks you are most accustomed to serve; but probably your minimum equipment will be:

    Cocktail glasses: they should be solid-stemmed, so that the hand will not warm the drink.

    Highball glasses: if you want them to double for Collinses and Juleps, get 14-ouncers with straight sides.

    Old-fashioned glasses: make sure they have heavy bottoms, so they'll stand up to your muddling machinations. These can be used for straight-drinkers, too, if you haven't shot- or drink-glasses.

    Sherry glasses: they can be pressed into extra service for liqueurs.

    Goblets: these can be used for wine, sours, flips.

    Never one to put a horse-blanket on a beautiful girl, Esquire puts thumbs down on coloured glasses which disguise the good looks of the drink itself. Only clear glass is in the clear with everyone but the camouflage experts.

13 *Trays* – if you haven't an official bar – whether it be a portable tucked into a corner of the living room or a real bar you can sit up to – you'll want an oversized tray to use for the purpose. Load it with liquor, bitters, fruit, necessary glasses and gadgets, ice bucket and carry it into the midst of the guests where you can make the drinks in plain sight. In any case, you'll want at least one tray for passing drinks, and collecting empties.

Cocktails

THE FIVE O'CLOCK
WHISTLE WHETTERS

Of the thousands of concoctions which slide down unsuspecting gullets in the fair name of cocktails, there are only a few which – year in, year out – rate encores and re-pours. Since you'll stir up a hundred Martinis, Manhattans or Old-Fashioneds to every fancy-handled 'drip drink', we arrange these aristocrats of good cheer – together with the companion-classic Daiquiri, Stinger and Champagne Cocktail – in Esquire's Goodtime Sip Parade, a compact section for your handy quick-reference.

Worthy of almost equal if less frequent respect are such good cocktails as the Sazarac, the Toddy, Ward Eight, Rum and Scotch Old-Fashioneds, Sours and the least repulsive of the Fizzes. These 'Good for a Change', invite you to experiment.

But there'll be times (your bartender should have told you) when you must steel yourself to mix up one of those fluffy, multicoloured abominations which, for some mysterious reason relating to iron-insides and paralysed palates, the 'ladies' insist upon downing. The habitual-offenders are there, unmanly drinks are segregated under 'Something for the Girls', where they can't interfere with your own tasteful toasting.

And then, for those occasions when you're possessed of a particular bottle of spirits and a random spirit of adventure, we've included a selected, alphabetised list of additional cocktails 'Something for the Boys'. No need to splash through pages of Caribbean cocktails when your cellar is down to its sole bottle of gin; just turn to the gin section and run your bar spoon down the list until something strikes your fancy.

MANHATTAN

2-1 MANHATTAN

3 dashes Orange Bitters

1/3 Italian Vermouth

2/3 Rye or Bourbon

Pour over ice cubes in tall glass, stir clockwise, chuck in a square piece of lemon rind, stir some more, then pour into chilled glass – with or without maraschino cherry.

4-1 MANHATTAN

4 parts Rye or Bourbon

1 part Italian vermouth

Stir, don't shake, with ice and pour into glass holding the proverbial cherry or, preferably, a twist of lemon peel.

DRY MANHATTAN

2 parts Rye or Bourbon

1 part French Vermouth

Stir gently with ice and pour into chilled cocktail glass. No cherry with this one.

THE OLD-FASHIONED

Them what like their Old-Fashioneds without sugar, without butters, without water or seltzer, without ice and certainly without fruit are just too old-fashioned to name their drink as 'straight whisky, please'.

OLD-FASHIONED

In a squatty, robust-bottomed tumbler of the type designed for and dedicated to this drink, place a lump of sugar. Wet this down with 3 dashes of Angostura bitters. (Some use 2 teaspoons of water, as well. Many prefer only 1 or 2 dashes bitters.) Crush the sugar with a wooden muddler, preferably one which has never been washed nor used for any less worthy purpose. Rotate glass so that sugar grains and bitters give it a lining, then add a crystal-clear lump of ice. Now pour in 1 1/2 oz bourbon or rye. Twist a bit of lemon peel over the top.

A Maraschino cherry, a slice of orange and a chunk of fresh or canned pineapple may be added; the drink may be given a final stir...but in both cases fall back for criticism from Old-Fashioned addicts.

Variation: add a dash of Curaçao. Try reducing sugar to 1/2 lump. Equal amount of granulated sugar may be used, but be sure to muddle.

ECCENTRIC OLD-FASHIONED

1 complete lemon peel

   squeezed into glass

1/2 teaspoon sugar

1/2 teaspoon Curaçao

2 ounces whisky

Shake well but do not strain and serve in glass garnished with slices of pineapple, orange and cherries.

MARTINI

VERY DRY MARTINI

'The Gibson'

1 part French Vermouth

5 parts Gin

Stir gently in tall glass with ice, strain into cocktail glass, add cocktail onion, twist a piece of lemon peel over each glass, then drop peel into Martini.

DRY MARTINI (1)

1 part French Vermouth

3 parts Gin

Dash of Orange Bitters

Stir without great heat in tall glass half-filled with broken ice, then pour into cocktail glass. Twist a small segment of lemon peel (1 inch by 1/2 inch) over the top then drop into glass.

DRY MARTINI (2)

1 part French Vermouth

2 parts Gin

Stir with ice in tall glass, until chilled. Serve in cocktail glass with a green olive or pearl onion. Twist piece of lemon peel on top.

MEDIUM MARTINI

1 part French Vermouth

1 part Italian Vermouth

2 parts Gin

Stir with ice in tall glass; strain into cocktail glass containing green olive.

SWEET MARTINI

Ladies Only

1 part Italian Vermouth

1 part Tom Gin

Dash of Orange Bitters

Stir with ice; serve with green olive. Twist piece of lemon peel on top.

Variations: For spirited occasions a few drops of Pernod, Oxygene or the local absinthe adds just the right touch to the dry Martini. Sticklers insist that a small pickled onion be used in lieu of the olive when absinthe is used. Maraschino, Benedictine, sprigs of mint, Crème de Menthe, orange peel and Angostura bitters are occasional 'third rails' for the gin-vermouth combination.

THE STINGER

Formerly a quiet member of the 'horsey' set, an also-ran in the cocktail derby, the Stinger buzzed into popularity when wartime pilots discovered how well it lives up to its name. Even though Army-Navy plane clothes have been doffed for plain clothes, the ex-fliers still like to check out on the Stinger. Flight Plan below:

STINGER

2 parts brandy

1 part white Crème de Menthe

Stir with cracked ice in tall mixing glass; strain into cocktail glass. The Stinger is sometimes served with a pair of short straws.

THE DAIQUIRI

Lime-and-rum of a Cuban sort was put on our social map by the Spanish-American War. A landing was made at Daiquiri near Santiago (the home of Bacardi), and the soldiers 'refreshed' themselves as though this were Ticonderoga – the glad news of their all round success spreading through the Army and Navy; since then our alliance with Ron de Cuba has been continuous and active. Thus:

DAIQUIRI COCKTAIL
Edition of 1898

Juice of half a lime

1 jigger (1½ oz) Bacardi rum, white

1 bar spoon powered sugar

Shake vimfully with cracked ice till shaker frosts; strain into cocktail glass.

FROZEN DAIQUIRI COCKTAIL
Modern Arctic-Tropic Edition

Juice of entire lime

2 oz Puerto Rican rum, white

1 teaspoon sugar

Assemble in an electric mixer, which is thereupon filled up with puffed-wheat-size ice. When almost frappéed, pour through large-meshed strainer into a 'saucer' champagne glass, allowing enough of the fine ice to tumble through to form a floe that would tempt a penguin. A dash (about 20 drops) of Cointreau is a crafty touch sometimes applied.

Variations on the theme: Some insist they form a more perfect union by adding a dash of white Maraschino liqueur; others interpolate a squirt of Triple Sec. Still others pink the whole situation up with Grenadine, in which case we are out of the Daiquiri category entirely but by no means in the bleak wilderness if bright eyes have anything to say about it. A particular cult even makes beige Daiquiris with Jamaican rum.

THE CHAMPAGNE COCKTAIL

Not a tipple to tender as a prelude to hamburgers and onions, the champagne cocktail is nonetheless such a lasting favourite with a certain genre of gals that you should have it in your collection. To make an impression (to say nothing of a dent in your budget), use a fine grade of dry champagne.

CHAMPAGNE COCKTAIL

Take a nice full-blown lemon and from it scrape off as much of the yellow as you can with a cube of sugar. Place the sweet in a champagne glass with a small lump of ice, add a dash of Angostura bitters and slowly fill the glass with champagne, stirring it only enough to dissolve the sugar. Serve with a twist of lemon peel.

GIMLET

The Gimlet is a sharp thirst-quencher and a mainstay of the British Empire in high-temperature lands East of Suez. You can also get a very decent Gimlet in London. At the Savoy it's made like so: 3 parts dry gin to 1 part Rose's lime juice. Shake with ice and strain into a large 4 oz cocktail glass. Add a dash of soda water for zip. A true Gimlet must be made with Rose's bottled lime juice, which vanished like nylons during the war but is now seen around again.

SILVER FIZZ

1 oz lemon juice

1 1/2 oz gin

1 teaspoonful sugar

1 egg white

Shake furiously with cracked ice, strain into highball glass, fill up with sparkling water. Give stirring rod a couple of twirls in it.

RAMOS, OR NEW ORLEANS FIZZ

Juices of 1/2 lime and 1/2 lemon

1 oz sweet cream

2 oz dry gin

White of one egg

3 dashes Orange Flower Water

Shake with vim and vigour amid cracked ice. Pour into tallish glass, which has been dunked upside down in a saucer of lemon juice and then in powdered sugar, add seltzer stingily (or none at all) lest there be too much dilution. (Note: Another recipe calls for 1/2 teaspoon powdered sugar. In any case, the secret is in long shaking. Twelve minutes is stated as the proper time.)

COLD TODDY

In the bottom of an Old-Fashioned glass, crush:

1/2 teaspoon sugar

1 strip lemon peel, about 1" long

1 teaspoon water

Add 1 or 2 cubes ice. Pour in 1 1/2-2oz of your favourite whisky, give it a quick stir, and there you are. You may add a bit of water or seltzer if you want to last longer.

SCOTCH OLD-FASHIONED

If you substitute Scotch Whisky for bourbon or rye, an earnest Scotch-lover's reaction will be, 'You've ruined some mighty fine Scotch.'

WARD EIGHT

Into a bar glass half filled with broken ice, put

1 teaspoon Grenadine

1 oz rye or bourbon

Juice of 1/2 lemon or 1/2 lime

Shake briskly and strain into cocktail glass. (Some use 1/2 lemon plus 1/2 teaspoon sugar. 1/2 pony of water is sometimes added.)

WHISKY SOUR

This is simply a species of fortified lemonade in concentrated form:

1 part lemon juice

1 spoonful sugar

3 parts bourbon or rye

Ice, stir and pour into short glass. Women like it decorated with fruit.

EL PRESIDENTE

The vanguard of Manhattan cognoscenti has discovered what regulars of El Chico in Greenwich Village have known for many a moon: the El Presidente cocktail is elixir for jaded gullets. Here's how George Stadelman makes it al El Chico:

Over ice in a tall mixing glass, pour:
- 1 oz white Cuban rum
- 1/2 oz orange Curaçao
- 1/2 oz dry vermouth
- Dash of Grenadine

Shake or stir well, then strain into cocktail glass. (When stirred instead of shaken, it will pour a delightfully clear, deep orange colour.) A twist of orange peel may be added.

BACARDI COCKTAIL

There used to be a club in Chicago where you could down one of these free if you asked for *Bac'*-ardi instead of Ba-*car'*-di, but no matter how you splice it, this rum drink is a favourite – particularly with the ladies.

1. AS SERVED AT THE BACARDI DISTILLERY, SANTIAGO

Juice of 1/2 lime
1 teaspoon sugar
1 1/2 oz Bacardi rum
Shake with very fine ice; strain into cocktail glass.

2. THE PINK KIND

Juice of 1 lime
1/2 teaspoon sugar
1 1/2 oz Bacardi rum
dash of Grenadine
Shake well with fine ice; strain into cocktail glass.

3. VARIATIONS ON THE THEME

Juice of half a lime
1 teaspoonful of Grenadine
1 part gin
2 parts Bacardi

BRANDY

THE SIDECAR

2/3 brandy
1/3 Cointreau
Dash of lime juice
Shake with very fine ice; strain into frosty cocktail glass.

SIDECAR (2)

(50 Million Frenchmen...)
1/3 lemon juice
1/3 Cointreau
1/3 cognac
Shake with cracked ice; strain.

ALEXANDER

1/2 jigger of gin

1/2 jigger of Crème de Cacao

1/2 jigger of cream

Ice, shake and serve in cocktail glass.

BRONX

2/3 jigger of gin

1/6 jigger French Vermouth

1/6 jigger Italian Vermouth

Dash of orange juice. Ice, shake well and serve in cocktail glass.

CLOVER CLUB

Squeeze juice of one lime into shaker

    Add white of one egg

    Two dashes of Grenadine

    1 1/2 jiggers of gin

Shake thoroughly and serve in cocktail glass.

ORANGE BLOSSOM

1/2 orange juice

1/2 Tom gin

PINK LADY

1 oz gin

1/2 oz applejack

White of one egg

Juice of 1/2 lime

Couple dashes of Grenadine, strawberry syrup or raspberry syrup

Shake vigorously with cracked ice. Strain. Sprig of mint optional decoration.

SLOE GIN FIZZ

1 jigger sloe gin

Juice one-half lemon

1 teaspoon powdered sugar

Shake well with ice, strain into highball glass and fill with soda. (Its hunting pink colour and fruity opulence are topped with a handsome collar of natural foam which, if the sloe gin be of first quality, is gladsome aplenty.)

GREEN FIZZ

2 oz gin

1 teaspoon sugar

1 teaspoon green Crème de Menthe

Juice 1 lemon

White of egg

Cracked ice

Shake well and serve

Perfect for the 'young innocent', pseudo or otherwise, the flip may be made with sherry or port in place of the brandy in this version:

THE FLIP

1 fresh egg yolk

1 teaspoon sugar

1 jigger brandy

Shake well. Serve in small wineglass. Sprinkle with nutmeg.

BOURBON AND RYE

Either bourbon or rye may be used in any of these cocktails, depending on your taste.

BRAINSTORM

1/4 French Vermouth

1/4 Benedictine

1/2 best rye whisky

Stir well with ice and float orange peel on top.

COMMODORE

1/3 bourbon whisky

1/3 Crème de Cacao

1/3 lemon juice

Dash of Grenadine syrup, serve in champagne glass. Tradition can be improved by the use of an electric mixer, with the resultant ice-floe similar to that of an Arctic-Tropic Daiquiri.

GLOOM LIFTER

Juice one-half lemon

1/2 spoon sugar

1/2 pony raspberry syrup

1/4 pony white of egg

1 jigger whisky

1/2 teaspoon brandy

HARRITY

Dash of bitters

1 dash gin

1 jigger whisky

HONOLULU

1/3 bourbon whisky

1/3 French Vermouth

1/3 Italian Vermouth

MCKINLEY'S DELIGHT

1 dash absinthe

2 dashes cherry brandy

2/3 whisky

1/3 Italian Vermouth

MILLIONAIRE COCKTAIL

1 1/2 oz whisky

1/2 oz Curaçao

1 dash Grenadine

White of 1 egg

Shake with ice as though 7 demons were goading you to it; strain into non-stingy cocktail glass.

SUBURBAN

Dash of orange bitters

Dash of bitters

1/5 port wine

1/5 Jamaica rum

3/5 whisky

WALDORF

Dash of bitters

1/3 whisky

1/3 absinthe

1/3 Italian Vermouth

WHISKY DAISY

1 jigger whisky

Juice of one-half lemon

3 dashes Cointreau or Curaçao

1 teaspoon sugar

Shake with fine ice, strain into 8 oz highball glass, fizz from siphon. Fruit garnish optional. May be served unstrained, with straws.

SCOTCH

In answer to the old complaint that there are not many ways of downing the gentlemen's drink except with water or soda, here are several satisfactory Scotch cocktails. It takes a Scotch drinker to appreciate them, though; they're not for the average cocktail taste.

ARTISTS' SPECIAL
(As served at Artist Bar in the Rue Pigalle, Paris)
1/2 Scotch whisky
1/2 sherry
1/6 lemon juice
1/6 Groseille syrup

THE BAIRN
1/3 Scotch whisky
1/3 Cointreau
1 dash orange bitters

BENEDICT
1/3 Scotch whisky
1/3 Benedictine
2/3 ginger ale

BORDEN CHASE
1/2 Scotch whisky
1/2 Italian Vermouth
1 dash of orange bitters
1 dash of Pernod or Oxygene

BUNNY HUG
(A dance of the period following World War 1)
1/3 gin
1/3 Scotch whisky
1/3 absinthe

CAMERON'S KICK
1/3 Scotch whisky
1/3 Irish whisky
1/6 lemon juice
1/6 Orgeat (almond) syrup

GENTLE JOHN
1 jigger Scotch whisky
1 dash of orange bitters, French Vermouth and Cointreau

GLAMIS
(pronounced Glarms)
1/2 Scotch whisky
1/2 Calisaya bitters

GLASGOW
1/2 Scotch whisky
1/2 French Vermouth
3 dashes absinthe
3 dashes bitters
Ice and shake well.

THE HEATHER
2/3 Scotch whisky
2 dashes of French Vermouth
1 dash of Angostura bitters

HIGHLAND BITTERS
One of the most famous of the authentic Scotch mixtures is called 'Highland Bitters' and is almost as old as the industry itself. Grind in a mortan the following:
1 3/4 oz gentian root
1/2 oz orange peel
1 oz coriander seed
1/4 oz camomile flowers
1/2 oz cloves
1/4 oz cinnamon.
Add this to two bottles of Scotch. let it stand for two weeks, sealed, in a crock or jar, then drink.

ROB ROY

2 parts Scotch whisky
1 part Italian vermouth
1 dash of bitters

ROBBER COCKTAIL

2/3 Scotch whisky
1/3 Italian Vermouth
Dash of bitters
Serve in cocktail glass with cherry

STONE FENCE

1 jigger of Scotch whisky
   in large glass
1 lump of ice
Fill with cider

TRILBY COCKTAIL

1/3 Scotch whisky
1/3 Parfait d'Amour
1/3 Italian Vermouth
2 dashes absinthe
2 dashes of orange bitters

GIN

ASYLUM COCKTAIL

1 part gin
1 part Pernod
Dash of Grenadine
Pour over large lumps of ice. Do not shake.

CHINA CLIPPER COCKTAIL

Conspicuous passenger:
   1 Chinese golden lim (These
   kumquats, preserved in syrup and
   put up in earthenware jars are
   obtainable at any Chinese shop or
   restaurant.)
   2/3 gin (yellow dry gin jibes best with
      the colour scheme)
   1/6 dry vermouth
   1/6 grapefruit juice
   2 shots orange bitters
   1 or 2 drops of the syrup of the
      kumquat
The liquid ingredients are stirred in a mixing glass with ice cubes and poured onto Miss Golden Lime, already in her glass cabin. Pleasant take-off!

CHOCOLATE SOLDIER

1/3 Dubonnet
2/3 gin
dash of lime juice

PALE DEACON

3 jiggers grapefruit juice
2 jiggers dry gin
1 dash of powdered sugar
Shake with cracked ice, serve in frosted glass.

DELMONICO

3/4 oz gin
1/2 oz of French Vermouth
1/2 oz Italian Vermouth
1/2 oz cognac
2 dashes Angostura
Twist of orange peel

GOLDEN DAWN

1/3 apple brandy
1/3 apricot brandy
1/3 dry gin
Dash of orange juice
Shake well, strain into cocktail glass; top with bar spoon of Grenadine, which will submarine to

the bottom of the glass and there stage a sunrise effect.

HEARST

One dash orange bitters
One dash Angostura bitters
^{1}/2 jigger Italian Vermouth
^{1}/2 jigger gin

MAIDEN'S PRAYER

(Served on the edge of the couch)

^{1}/4 dry gin
^{1}/4 Cointreau
^{1}/4 lemon juice
Dash of orange bitters

Ice and shake well

PRAIRIE CHICKEN

1 pony of gin
1 egg in claret glass
Pepper and salt

Cover top with gin and serve

RACQUET CLUB

Dash of orange bitters
^{1}/2 gin
^{1}/2 French Vermouth
Orange peel

TEXSUN RANGER

^{1}/4 Texsun grapefruit
1 teaspoon Maraschino
^{1}/3 sweet vermouth
^{1}/3 dry vermouth
^{1}/3 dry gin

VIRGIN

^{1}/3 Forbidden Fruit
^{1}/3 white Crème de Menthe
^{1}/3 gin

Shake well and strain

THE CONNECTICUT BULLFROG

The ingredients are awful but the result does have something.

4 parts gin
1 part New England rum
1 part lemon juice
1 part maple syrup

Shake these ingredients together until your arms ache. Then have someone else do the same thing with about ten times the usual amount of ice. Serve frappé. All your guests will gratefully swear that they are at the Waldorf Astoria.

FLORADORA

Juice one-half lime
^{1}/2 teaspoon sugar
^{1}/2 pony raspberry syrup
1 jigger gin

Frappé, fizz with ginger ale and serve in a Tom Collins glass.

FREE SILVER

Juice one-quarter lemon
^{1}/3 spoon sugar
^{2}/3 gin
^{1}/3 Jamaica rum
^{1}/2 pony milk

Ice, shake and serve in a tall glass, fill up with soda.

KISS THE BOYS GOODBYE

^{1}/2 sloe gin
^{1}/2 brandy
^{1}/2 white of egg
Juice of 1 lemon

Shake very well with plenty of ice and strain.

RUM COCKTAILS

RUM SOUR

3/4 oz lemon juice

1/4 teaspoon sugar

1 1/4 golden lightbodied rum

Shake with ice; give glass a 'lid' of 151 proof rum.

COOL O' THE EVENING

Crush thoroughly 1 sprig mint in shaker. Add juice 1/2 lemon, 1/2 teaspoon sugar, 1 jigger white rum, cracked ice. Shake till heavy frost. Strain into cocktail stemmer. (No fresh mint? Then use couple drops *white* Crème de Menthe.)

EYE-OPENER

Liqueur glass of old Haitian rum

Teaspoon Grenadine

Yolk of one egg

2 dashes of Curaçao

2 dashes of apricot brandy

Ice and shake well.

HAITIAN COCKTAIL

1 jigger Haitian rum

1 jigger fresh lime juice

1 spoon powdered sugar

Ice, shake and serve in cocktail glass.

HARPO'S SPECIAL

2 oz rum

1 drop bitters

1.2 teaspoon Curaçao

Juice of one-half lemon

1/2 teaspoon sugar

Shake well and strain.

HONEY BEE

1 part honey

4 parts Bacardi

1 part lemon juice

Mix well, then add ice and shake.

RUM ORANGE COCKTAIL

1/4 orange juice

1/4 Italian Vermouth

1/2 Bacardi

1 pinch powdered cinnamon

Ice, shake well, and serve in cocktail glass.

COMMODORE

1/2 teaspoon sugar

One dash lemon juice

White of one egg

One drink of Bacardi rum

1 dash of Grenadine

1 dash of raspberry syrup

SUICIDE COCKTAIL

1 dollop of Haitian rum

1/2 dollop Crème de Cacao

1 dollop White Rock

1 Cryst-O-Mint Life Saver dropped from a great height.

(In preparing this drink, the glass is placed on the floor and the mixer stands erect, holding the Life Saver at shoulder height. If he misses the glass three times in a row, he does not need another drink – not very badly, anyway.)

SUNSHINE COCKTAIL

Equal parts pineapple juice, dry vermouth, white rum. Dash of Grenadine. Stir with cracked ice.

WHAT'S IT?

White of one egg

1/2 jigger Jamaica rum

1/2 jigger port wine

Ice, shake, serve in eight-ounce glass, fill up with soda.

ARISE MY LOVE

Put 1 teaspoon Crème de Menthe in a champagne glass, then fill with champagne.

Ernest Hemingway's
DEATH IN THE AFTERNOON COCKTAIL

Pour 1 jigger of absinthe into a champagne glass.
Add iced champagne until it attains the proper opalescent milkiness.
Drink 3 to 5 of these slowly.

DUBONNET

1 glass Dubonnet
1/2 glass lemon syrup
Balance soda water

On the blonde side, there's GOLDEN FRAPPÉ constructed with one glass of white port (in case you aren't acquainted with this wine type, now's the time!), one glass of orange juice, two tablespoons sugar; stir till sugar is dissolved, then pour over finely crushed ice in a quartet of tallish tumblers. (And how beautifully those bullfrogs are singing this evening. Like parched nightingales.)

MARCONI WIRELESS

Two dashes orange bitters
1/3 Italian Vermouth
2/3 applejack

MERRY WIDOW

1/2 French Vermouth
1/2 Dubonnet

Fruit of the hen figures cheerily in the perennially apropos PORT FLIP over which country-clubbers cast an appreciative lip. Its formula, as your great grandsire could have told you, calls for the contents of two eggs, cracked on the rim of a shaker, two teaspoons sugar, one cup of port, much, much cracked ice; shaken dementedly. Pour into two Delmonico glasses or fair sized goblets. Freckle with nutmeg.

SENSATION

2 parts port wine
1 part brandy
Twist of lemon peel
Stir well and serve.

SHERRY COCKTAIL

2 parts dry sherry, pre-chilled
2 parts French Vermouth pre-chilled

SHERRY OLD-FASHIONED

With the full trappings of an Old-Fashioned – the lump of sugar, thrice shot with Angostura and muddled till dissolved; twist of lemon epidermis, double jigger sherry, ice cube or two; Maraschino cherry, orange slice, glass baton; and serve pronto before the melting of the ice undermines authority.

VERMOUTH SPECIAL

1/2 teaspoon sugar
1 lemon peel squeezed into glass
1 dash bitters
1 sprig mint
1/2 teaspoon Curaçao
1 teaspoon Amer Picon
2 oz Italian Vermouth
1 oz whisky
Shake well with ice, strain, serve.

BRANDY AND CORDIALS IN COCKTAILS

BRANDY DAISY

2 oz brandy

$1/2$ oz Grenadine

Juice of 1 lemon

Shake with finely cracked ice; pour unstrained into ample highball glass; decorate with fruits ad lib. Harpoon with straw.

BRANDY SOUR

$1 1/2$ oz brandy

Juice of half a lemon

1 teaspoon sugar

One to three dashes of Angostura

Shake with cracked ice. Strain into glass, preferably Delmonico. May be cargoed with orange slice and a cherry.

CAFÉ COCKTAIL

1 black coffee

$1/2$ Crème de Cacao

$1/2$ cognac

1 teaspoonful sugar

Lemon peel

Shake well, strain and serve

CHAMPAGNE DES PAUVRES

1 glass of brandy

$1/2$ glass lemon syrup

APPLE BRANDY COCKTAIL

4 parts apple brandy

1 part Grenadine

1 part juice of lemon or lime

Agitate coolly and sieve.

BETWEEN-SHEETS

$1/3$ cognac

$1/3$ Crème de Cacao

$1/3$ cream

1 dash bitters

1 teaspoon sugar

Lemon peel

Plenty cracked ice

Shake well, strain and serve.

BLACKJACK

1 pony Kirsch

1 dash brandy

1 pony coffee

Frappéed with fine ice. Any of these will bring out the figure-skating-champ instincts in you.

BOSOM CARESSER

$1/6$ Curaçao

$1/6$ brandy

$1/3$ Madeira

1 teaspoon Grenadine

1 yolk of egg

BRANDY COCKTAIL

Use 10oz glass

Cracked ice

1 sprig of mint

1 lemon peel, squeezing juice in glass

$1/2$ teaspoon sugar

1 drop bitters

$1/2$ teaspoon Curaçao

2 oz cognac

Shake lightly, strain and serve.

BRANDY CRUSTAS

(as served at Harry's Bar, Paris)

Take a small wine glass, moisten the rim with lemon, dip the rim of the glass into caster sugar. Peel the rind of half a lemon and fit this curl of peel into the contour of your glass. Then in a shaker, mix 1 teaspoon of sugar, 3 dashes of Maraschino, 3 dashes of bitters, juice of one-quarter lemon, 1 glass brandy. Shake well and pour into a prepared glass.

FULL HOUSE

Dash of bitters
1/3 yellow Chartreuse
1/3 Benedictine
1/3 apple whisky

GIN WITH COINTREAU

Gin 1 jigger; juice of 1/2 lime; white of 1 egg; Grenadine 1 dash. Shake and strain into wine glass whose rim has been sugar-frosted.

HARVARD

Dash of orange bitters
2/5 jigger brandy
3/5 Italian Vermouth (stir)
Fill from chilled siphon

HOP FROG

1/3 brandy
2/3 lime juice
Ice and shake

JACK ROSE COCKTAIL

1 1/2 oz apple brandy
1/2 oz grenadine
Juice of one-half lemon or lime
Shake with cracked ice; strain.

KIRSCH AND CASSIS

1 glass Cassis
1/2 glass Kirsch
Balance soda water

MY SIN COCKTAIL

1 oz absinthe
1 oz anisette
1 drop bitters
White of egg
Plenty of ice, shake well and strain.

QUEEN ELIZABETH

1/4 Benedictine
1/2 French Vermouth
1/4 lime juice

STIRRUP CUP

1 jigger cherry brandy
1 jigger brandy
Juice of half lemon

TROPICAL COCKTAIL

1 dash of bitters
1 dash of orange bitters
1/3 Crème de Cacao
1/3 Maraschino
1/3 French Vermouth

TURF COCKTAIL

2 dashes orange bitters
2 dashes Maraschino
2 dashes absinthe
1/2 French Vermouth
1/2 gin
Shake well, ice, and serve with olive.

WEDDING BELLS

1/6 cherry brandy
1/6 orange juice
1/3 gin
1/3 Dubonnet

WHITE LADY

2/3 Cointreau
1/6 Crème de Menthe
1/6 brandy

BLUE MOON

2/3 gin
1/3 French Vermouth
1 dash orange bitters
1 dash of Crème Yvette

DOLORES

1/3 cherry brandy
1/3 Crème de Cacao
1/3 Spanish brandy
White of one egg

DREAM

1/3 Curaçao
2/3 brandy
Dash absinthe

GRENADINE COCKTAIL

1 teaspoon Framboise syrup
1/3 Oxygene cusenier
1/3 gin
1/3 white mint
Shake well and strain into cocktail glass.

GYPSY

2/3 vodka
1/3 Benedictine
1 dash of bitters

MAIDEN'S KISS

1/5 Crème de Roses
1/5 Curaçao
1/5 Maraschino
1/5 yellow Chartreuse
1/5 Benedictine

MORNING AFTER

1 white of egg
1 teaspoonful anisette syrup
1 glass absinthe
Dash of soda on top

NIGHT CAP

1 yolk egg
1/3 anisette
1/3 Curaçao
1/3 brandy

PLUIE D'OR

1/3 gin
1/3 vieille cure
1/6 Curaçao
1/6 Kummel

PRINCE GEORGE

1/3 Grand Marnier
2/3 Bacardi
Juice of one-half lime; twist
   of lemon peel

WIDOW'S KISS

1/3 Parfait d'Amour
1/3 yellow chartreuse
1/3 Benedictine
White of egg floated on top

NETHERLAND COCKTAIL

1 oz. Brandy
1 oz. Curaçao
Dash orange bitters
Stir amid cracked ice. Strain.

PUMPKIN COACH COCKTAIL

2 parts liqueur Cesoriac
1 part vermouth
1 part cherry juice
3 limes (to each pint)
Slathers of ice (or you will be
   going home in a basket).

VALENCIA

2/3 apricot brandy
1/3 orange juice
2 dashes orange bitters

Wines

THE DRINK OF THE GODS

Wine has been a prop for every major love scene since Aeschylus dubbed the gleaming goblet the 'mirror of the heart' – why not at *yours?*

Wine has worked its flavour-magic at the tables of the great from time immemorial – making a feast of fine food, adding a welcome pick-up even to dull provender – so why not at your table?

Don't be intimidated by wine-lovers' mumbo-jumbo about vintage years, intricate serving rituals, do's and don'ts in dealing with the previous stuff the vintners sell. The 'right wine' is simply a matter of opinion; the 'rules' are nothing but majority opinion on how best to bring out the flavour of wines and their accompanying foods. Besides, many of those 'rules', based on the selection and service of the great vintage European wines, are just so much excess baggage when it comes to buying and enjoying New World or contemporary-style wines, 'Vintage year,' for example, means nothing to a California wine; reliable climate spares the American wine industry those off-years which makes one in three European harvests a dud. State and federal laws combine with American marketing methods to assure standard flavour and character for each brand, thus eliminating another area of margin-or-error guesswork that sometimes plagues the buyer of other wines.

In fact, the whole business of buying and serving wines has become so much simpler in recent years that no one need quiver at the snobbish shrine of old. Take the 'rules' or leave 'em – but don't miss the real pleasure that wine adds to your meal (nor the aura of romance that the wine bottle brings to your table for two!).

But like Lord Chesterfield's gentleman, who by definition is never rude unintentionally, you'd do well to know the rules before you break them.

There are two major classes of wines – table wines and appetiser or dessert wines.

TABLE WINES result when the pure juice of the grape is allowed to ferment naturally and completely; their alcoholic content is less than 14% by volume. They may be red or white, still or sparkling (effervescent), but the natural and complete fermentation uses up most of the grape sugar so they are usually dry (dry means the opposite of sweet). And there you have the reason for their fine suitability for the table: unless you like Coca-Cola with fish or candy with steak, you wouldn't want a sweet wine with your dinner.

APPETISER AND DESSERT WINES result when the natural fermentation process is stopped before completion by the addition of grape brandy. This not only ups the alcoholic content to 17-21%, but also preserves some of the natural grape sugar, making a sweetish wine. Sherry, muscatel and port are the best-known among these brandy-fortified wines.

A third category is made up of aromatised wines like Vermouth, but since they are used mainly in mixed drinks or as aperitifs they concern bartenders more than cooks.

Within each class, of course, there is a profusion of names and fames. If you have a reliable dealer, you may be able to get along very well simply by asking for 'a light red wine' or 'a dry white wine' or whatever class your needs dictate. Within each class you will then learn the various types: claret and burgundy, say, among the still red wines for table use...Chablis and Sauternes among the whites. But those names, which merely indicate wine-*types* in America, all come from Europe, where the name is a virtual birth certificate, thus it's a good idea to know something of European wines, if only to understand what the names on other wines infer.

Here is a run-down on the best known wines, followed by comparable information which may help you in selecting the best American wines which have borrowed European names.

WINES OF FRANCE
The most celebrated French wine districts are:

BORDEAUX

Wines grown in that section of France surrounding the old Gascon seaport, on the Gironde River, are all called Bordeaux, but they range from the fresh white Graves to the full red St Emilion or Pomerol. Of the eight wine districts of Bordeaux, the three most famous are Medoc, Graves and Sauternes. Medoc is the home of most of the great clarets – dry, light, delicate red table wines. Chateau Lafite Rothschild and Chateau Margaux are the greatest of these. Graves produces several great red wines (Chateau Haut Brion, for example) as well as pleasant whites which are reasonably dry. Sauternes are medium-sweet white wines recommended for use with dessert; Chateau Yquem and Chateau Latour Blanche are most honoured among sauternes.

Bordeaux wines are shipped to the world under three main types of labels: Chateau bottling, wine of a definite vintage produced from grapes grown on an estate and bottled there; Monopole or Trade Mark brand of shipper, a blend of wines from a small number of similar vineyards, and finally Parish or District labels, wines blended from several vinyards and often of several vintages.

Except for the great Chateau wines of extraordinary vintages, the Monopole or Parish labels of a reliable shipper are usually a better buy; a shipper's reputation depends wholly on the quality of these wines.

BURGUNDY

The ancient Duchy of Burgundy, long famous for its wines, offers both red and white wines. The red wines are dry, full-bodied and fruity. The white wines are very dry and quite thin when compared with those of Bordeaux. Most of the Burgundy wine available in America is shipped under the name of the Parish or district where it was produced, although some wine has come over under the vineyard name as Estate Bottled wine.

Best known names in Burgundy are Chambertin, Romanée-Conti, La Romanée, Corton, Clos de Vougeot, Macon, Beaujolais and Pommard in red wines; and Chablis, Pouilly, Meursault and Montrachet in white wines. A quantity of sparkling wine, red and white, is produced in Burgundy.

CHAMPAGNE

The finest sparkling wine in the world is produced from wines made from black grapes grown in a strictly limited area that comprises the Old Province of Champagne – in the northeast corner of France, now called the Department of the Marne. Although sparkling wines are made all over the world wherever grapes grow, and many of them are labelled 'champagne', none has ever equalled the lightness, delicacy, finesse or character of true champagne. Since it takes 10 to 15 years to prepare the best champagne for market, there is no such thing as a bargain champagne. It is truly the 'drink of the gods'.

Champagne in its natural state is perfectly dry, but many varieties have a sweet liqueur added in the last states of preparation. The French labels indicate the amount of sweetness added, like this: Nature (no sweetening added) ...Brut (up to 1% sweetening)...Extra Dry (up to 3% sweetening)...Sec or Dry (up to 5% sweetening)...Doux (up to 12% sweetening).

Since champagne is usually a blend of several wines from different vineyards, the best buying guide is the blender's reputation. Here are just a few of the finest producers: Charles Heidsieck, Pol Roger, Pommery and Greno, Veuve Clicquot, Louis Roedereer, G. H. Mumm and Co., Bouche Fils.

VOUVRAY

Light and quite sweet are the wines of the Valley of Loire. They are very delicate and do not always travel well, consequently, they are not well known outside of France. There is a sparkling Vouvray which is like a sweet champagne, and even the still wines are mildly effervescent.

COTE DU RHONE

Wines from the Rhone Valley – south of Burgundy and toward the Mediterranean – are distant cousins of Burgundies. The reds are a deeper hue – almost purple – the whites pack an unexpected punch. The best known are Cote Rotie, red;

Hermitage, red, white and straw-coloured; Chateau Neuf-du-Pape, red, the traditional beverage of the Avignon Popes; and Tavel, a pinkish wine.

ALSACE

Wines produced in this redeemed province on the French side of the Rhine resemble the German more than the French wines; Alsace forms the southern fringe of the Rhine vineyard region. Alsation Rhine wine is dry, fruity, flowery; other wines of Alsace are names varietally: Riesling, Tokay, Sylvaner, Traminer, etc., after the grape variety themselves.

WINES OF GERMANY

The two principal wine-producing districts of Germany are the valleys of the Rhine and the Moselle rivers, with their tributary streams, the Main and the Naha (to the Rhine) and the Saar and the Ruwer (to the Moselle). Although both white and red wines are produced, it is only the whites which are renowned – and they rank almost equal to the French wines. *Rhine* wines are usually very dry and light, with a delicate bouquet. *Moselle* wines are still very dry and light, with a delicate bouquet. Moselle wines are still lighter, have a more flowery bouquet. They also have a tang that gives the impression of a slight sparkling quality on the tongue.

Names of Rhine wines to remember are: Hochheimer, Niersteiner, Rudesheimer, Liebfraumilch and Steinberger. Moselle wines to remember are Zeltinger, Brauneberger, Piesporter, Bernkasteler. Polysyllabic words on labels can be a help in intelligent ordering, if you've the patience to study them out: *auslese* means made from selected bunches of grapes...*beerenaulese* means made from selected individual grapes from selected bunches (and it also means the wine is going to be very expensive!)...*spätlese* means that the grapes were allowed to hang on the vine until covered with a mould – to make a sweet and alcoholic wine – *naturwein* or *Ungezuckerter Wein* means made from ripe but not overripe grapes, thus comparatively dry...*edelberren* indicates that the grapes were overripe...*trockenberrenauslese* means you're in for the rare treat; this wine is made only once in 5 or 10 years, from selected semi-dried grapes; it's sweet, and dear...*cabinet* is applied to any wine which is the finest of its kind.

WINES OF ITALY

Italy is said to be one large vineyard. The best known red table wines from Italy are Chianti, Barolo, Barbera, Nebbiolo (sometimes sparkling); whites include Orevieto, Est!! Est!!, Asti Spumante. But probably the Italian wine best liked and most used outside Italy itself is the red Chianti from Tuscany. Chianti is in its prime five or six years after vintage – so look for dust on the familiar straw-covered bottle!

AMERICAN WINES

American wines imported to Europe, are not allowed to feature the European name. Instead they carry their own provenance and, usually, a brief description of style. That's why it may be helpful, in choosing among the myriad American wines, to know these general facts:

1 Grapes for dessert wines must be ripened to a high sugar content, so hot sunshine is indicated. Interior valleys and southern part of California provide said hot sunshine in large quantities – so 'Fresno Valley', 'Southern California', 'San Joaquin' or 'Sacramento Valley' are good signs on a sherry or port label.

2 Grapes for table wines should be developed to fruit acidity rather than fruit sweetness, so the cooler weather of the northern coast of California or the eastern states is more appropriate. Most notable are grapes from the vicinity of San Francisco: the Sonoma, Napa and Santa Clara districts.

3 California vineyards are based on transplanted European vines, so California wines bear a close resemblance to the Old World product. But the harsher climes of Ohio, New York and the 24 other wine-producing states of the United States require hardier vines; so wines from states other than California, made from American grapes, are distinctly different from the European; they should be enjoyed as the unique wines they are, not subjected to unfair comparison.

DESSERT WINES

SPAIN

Sherry from Jerez has never been successfully imitated elsewhere in the world. See 'Apéritifs' section for a description of the various types – and remember Oloroso when you want an unusual after-dinner wine.

Spain's second claim to wine fame is Malaga, an 18% alcohol wine which is very sweet, walnut-coloured and sprung from Muscat grapes. The most famous of its three types is Lacimra Christi – for which grapes are dried in the sun, their precious juices captured, and their fortified wine product mixed with another heavy and sweet wine. Another type is Moscato. Malaga gets better and better as it gets older and older; it has been stored for centuries without deterioration!

PORTUGAL

Along the upper reaches of the Duro River, the steep banks stretch back on both sides, entirely covered by vineyards that produce the grapes from which true port is made. Most Port is ruby-red, although a small amount of white Port is made; and most Port is a blended wine, but there are 'Vintage ports' of exceptional years.

These are the four general types of Port:

1. RUBY

The gay dog. Red as its name and lusty as it looks. Rich, full-bodied, fruity, slightly astringent. But don't develop into a Three Bottle Man or you'll get out. Serve at room temperature.

2. TAWNY

Older, milder, subtler. Less sweet. The colour ranges, according to age, from purplish brown ('medium') to topaz yellow (extremely old). For epicures and invalids. Served chilled.

3. WHITE

Actually yellow. Made from white grapes. Best when old and dry, to be served chilled to wash down your pre-dinner caviar and rattlesnakes.

4. VINTAGE

Product of a specially declared 'Vintage Year', kept separate from wines of ordinary years. Gains its maturity in bottle instead of in cask. Takes a Jeeves to open it. Serve at baronial-hall temperature.

MADEIRA

On the little island off Portugal, the famous Madeira wine is grown – rich, nutty, brown-coloured and potent. Madeira wines lack standardization. Making it is a business of collecting new wines pressed from a dozen kinds of grapes grown in every conceivable sort of tiny vineyard, subjecting them to hot-storage treatment in an estufa (substitute for old-fashioned trip to Indies and back), fortifying them with 10% extra alcohol, toning them with older and different wines, and thereafter touching them up with a bit of this and that during the course of a generation or so.

The nearest one can come to a classification is to say that:

Malmsey is the most honeyedly luscious and should be served with dessert and after. Also good at tea time with wafers or cake.

Bual (or Boal) is the medium-sweet; safe choice when you don't know your guests' preferences. Serve any time.

Sercial is the distinctly dry one, a bit strange and unaccountable at first sip; but at second sip you begin wondering how much there is in the house. Serve before dinner or with the first course.

Soleras are very old wines (all types) that have been kept up to their spark by the judicious addition of younger ones.

All Madeira wines are best served slightly cool, not cold. The island's winter climate during the duke and duchess season give you the hint – it's 61F.

SICILY

The island of Sicily produces Marsala, a Madeira-like wine which is mildly fortified. It tastes a bit like sherry, but is richer, more mellow. Its varieties are designated as:

Virgin – not fortified with brandy, but nonetheless 19% or more alcohol by volume

S.O.M. – Superior Old Marsala
O.P. – Old Particular
L.P. – London Particular
O.S. – Old Solera

An especially sweet Muscatel is also produced in Sicily – a natural sweet wine suitable for dessert use. The Sicilian Malvasia is fortified.

HUNGARY

Hungary's most famous wine is Tokay – a sweet, pungent wine which is the product of natural fermentation of perfectly dried grapes. the drier is called Szamorodni and the sweet Azzu.

HOW TO SERVE WINES

After you've sipped enough wines to be able to form your own judgements, you may decide that wine is at its best when it's drunk from the bottle or watered with ice cubes or taken by injection. But until that time when you can indulge your own preferences on the basis of your own experience, you may want to be guided by the men who know the Bacchus-brew best: the wine experts. Their common-sense advice for uncommon enjoyment of table wines can be boiled down to three:

1 Red wines are best with red meat, white wines with white meats, fish and fowl. Champagne goes with everything. (Practically any good wine goes with practically any good dish, but if you went at it blindly you would probably discover that a light ethereal white seems inadequate for a ruddy roast beef or steak, while an opulent-bodied Burgundy is apt to overpower the delicate flavour of fresh fish. Switched, these combinations would be perfect.) That colour-scheme 'rule' makes for easy memory, but if you would be more specific here's a list to ignore:
Aperitif – (Sherry, the foreign aperitifs or stand cocktails. Refer to the chapter on cocktails)
Hors D'Oeuvre – Dry white, Chablis, Sauternes
Oysters – Chablis, Sauternes or Champagne

Soup – Chablis or Sauternes

Fish – Chablis, Sauternes, Moselle, Alsatian

Entree – Light meats, chicken, etc. – White Burgundy; Pouilly or Chablis, Rhine wines

Game – Red Burgundies: Chambertins, Pommards

Roasts – Red Bordeaux; red Burgundies, Claret

Dessert – Champagne or White Bordeaux, Chateau Yquem

Cheese, Fruit or Nuts – Burgundy or Claret (Stilton takes port) or fortified wines like Madeira, port, sweet sherry.

Coffee – Brandy (cordials for women)

2 One table-wine is sufficient for all but a formal dinner, but if more than one wine is to be served during the course of the meal the heavier, fuller-bodied wines should follow the lighter and more delicate – which usually means that reds follow whites. Sweet wines are reserved for last – with the dessert. However, it is perfectly correct to serve champagne as a dessert wine, even though a heavier wine has been previously served during the dinner.

3 Red wines are generally served at room temperature, while whites are chilled – but all sparkling wines are served chilled. To be more explicit the drinks listed below should all be chilled:

Champagnes	Sparkling Burgundies
Carbonates	Still Whites
Dry Sherries	Vermouths
Aperitif Wines	

All still Reds at room temperature. (Or slightly chilled if you prefer.)

Ice is never put into the wine itself, of course. To chill, place in the refrigerator for an hour or so, or set the bottle in a bucket of ice for 20 to 30 minutes. To bring to room temperature, put the wine on the dining table a few hours before dinner. Never warm wine artificially. Beyond that, it's a question of niceties like these:

Preferred wine glasses are colourless, so the wine's colour is not obscured, and stemmed, so the hand does not warm the wine. You can get by very nicely with simple 5–6oz stemmers to be used for all table wines, plus 3–4 ounces for dessert and appetiser wines.

Wine should be poured slowly, so that any sediment which may have settled is not disturbed. The host usually pours a little in his own glass before filling his guest's glasses, just in case a bit of cork spills out with the first pour. Wine glasses are customarily filled only partially, so that the full fragrance will gather in the glass between wine-level and brim.

Connoisseurs say that smoking interferes drastically with the enjoyment of wine (as it does with food) – possible exception is sherry. And, of course, wine is meant to be sipped for its own sake, not gulped for thirst's sake.

HOW TO STORE WINES

For *all wines,* avoid sunlight, shock and temperature changes. Fifty-five to sixty degrees is best for wine storage, but if that's not possible, try for a constant temperature in any case.

For *table wines*: store all wine having 14% alcohol or less on its side, preferably with the bottom of the bottle a bit higher than the mouth, so that the cork will be kept moist by the wine. This keeps the cork expanded, tightly sealing the bottle, and thus eliminates the danger of Invasion by Air. Once opened, table wine should be stored in the refrigerator; left open and at room temperature it will turn to vinegar, sometimes within a day or so.

For *fortified wines*: store dessert and appetiser wines in an upright position, preferably standing so that one bottle can be removed from the shelf without disturbing the others.

If you have room, it's a good idea to lay down a cellar. Many wines improve (and increase in value) after a lay-away period...buying by the case means economy...and a handy source of supply is a convenience as well as a connoisseur's delight. The apartment dweller can often manage a 'cellar' by way of a sturdy wooden cabinet or a honeycomb of shelves in a closet. The home owner has a natural in his basement, in any even-temperatured, dark spot away from the furnace.

If you are going about accumulating wines that will be a practical adjunct to your living and not merely a hobby to exhibit to friends, it is well to begin with your needs. Take your typical menu to an unimpeachable dealer and let him start you off on your taste tests. Sample a different wine each week and gradually arrive, by elimination, at the types that suit you best. When you hit on a good one, buy in quantity for your cellar.

Aperitifs

CONTINENTAL COCKTAILS

In addition to the 'spirited' appetiser known as cocktail, there is a wine-based contribution to the cocktail-hour known as the aperitif. A companionable beverage, getting along harmoniously with the various viands to follow, the aperitif rarely exceeds an alcoholic tally of 18-20% by volume, compared to the cocktails 20–90%. The wise host always has one such 'continental cocktail' to offer, along with his more potent potables.

Although the French consider Pernod and Oxygene aperitifs, the Hungarians drink Szamorodni, and other national groups go in for Aquavit, Lillet, Tequila, Rojena, vodka and so on. The Big Four aperitifs are:

1. SHERRY

True sherries, wines grown in and around Jerez, Spain, fall Into four main classes: *palido* (full bodied, of medium colour and dryness); *fino* (very pale, light, dry and delicate); *amontillado* (pale, very dry, a perfect aperitif); and *oloroso* (deeper-coloured, nutty-flavoured, best for after-dinner use). The other names you will run across include amoroso, a pale, golden, medium sherry of the *palido* class; *manzanilla*, thin and dry with a bitter flavour; *vina de pasto*, so dry and light it is used as a table wine; *montilla*, very pale and extremely dry when old, with something of an *amontillado* flavour.

Very dry sherries should be chilled to 50F.; medium sherries such as *amoroso* should be slightly chilled and rich *olorosos* improve if the bottle is opened and left standing at room temperature. All are served in a pipe-stem, V-shaped 2 oz. glass.

2. VERMOUTH

Italian vermouth is made from aged and blended white wines infused with some 25 or 30 herbs and fortified with brandy to about 16% alcoholic strength. Of the many varieties, the most seen are the standard (containing a good deal of sugar and about 15% alcohol, usually drunk straight)...vermouth bianco (a white vermouth, very sweet, which is a favourite with the fair sex)... and the dry (which has zabout 18% of alcohol by volume). Serve it:

ICED AND WITH SODA

Fill a large goblet $1/2$ or $2/3$ full of vermouth, add several lumps of ice and a small amount of soda. Good before and during lunch as well as in the cocktail hour.

CHILLED AND STRAIGHT

Blend French and Italian varieties to suit your palate, chill but don't ice, and serve in a regular cocktail glass. Add a twist of lemon if you're in the mood.

THE AMERICANO

3 oz. Italian Vermouth

Dash of bitters

Slice of lemon peel

Seltzer as desired

Serve in a small highball glass or goblet.

French vermouth, a blend of fine white wines fortified with spirits and aromatised with some 40 herbs, is pale and dry, lacking the sweetness of the darker Italian product. Its characteristic taste is due to the fact that its wine-base is aged in much the same way that sherry is treated – left in butts out in the sun and rain for at least 2 years.

3. BYRRH

(rhymes with 'her')

The juice of sweet and dry grapes is mixed, then passed over a series of aromatic plants and Peruvian bark to produce this aperitif of stimulating taste and aroma. It is served... frappéed, in a cocktail glass chilled, in a wine glass with ice and water or soda, in a highball glass as byrrh-cassis.

BYRRH-CITRON

3 oz. byrrh

1/2 oz. lemon syrup

Soda or plain water to taste

Serve in highball glass with lump of ice.

4. DUBONNET

A blend of carefully selected old 'liqueur' wines to which Peruvian bark or quinine is added. It has a rich, slightly sweet flavour with the qualities of a mild liqueur. Serve it...

...well chilled in a small sherry or cocktail glass

...with soda or water and ice in a highball glass, or as a

DUBONNET COCKTAIL

1/2 Dubonnet

1/2 gin

Slice of lemon

Stir with ice and strain into cocktail glass. (Whisky, sherry, vermouth or rum may be used in place of gin; the combinations are legion.)

P.S.: People who like to make rules say that aperitifs should always be chilled, should never be served with anything more imposing than plain salted crackers or cheese wafers and should always be sipped, not gulped. We say: do what you like, so long as you like it!

After-dinner Drinks

CORDIALLY YOURS

After a good meal, a good liqueur – to aid digestion and conversation as well as to clear the palate for further drinking. Gourmets groan at the thought of following a heavy meal with anything but brandy, others claim almost equal rights for Crème de Menthe, each country has its favourite cordial – and so the question of an after-dinner tipple turns out to be dealer's choice. Since cordials increase as rapidly as rabbits, it is almost impossible to give a full listing...but here are the sturdy ones which have survived for centuries. Let your palate (and your purse) prevail!

ABSINTHE
Liquorice-tasting powerhouse, now illegal but agreeably replaced by Pernod or Oxygene.

ADVOCAAT
A thick cordial from Holland, often called 'egg brandy', made of eggs, sugar and brandy.

ANISETTE
Made from anise seeds (from France).

APRICOT LIQUEUR
Choice dried apricots distilled with fine old cognac. Very popular.

AQUAVIT
Danish version of kummel, caraway seed flavour predominates.

ARRAK
Flavoured with anise (from the Near East).

BENEDICTINE
Proprietary formula, from France.

CALISAY
The national liqueur of Spain, brandy with two per cent quinine, flavoured with Peruvian bark.

CALVADOS
French version of American apple-jack.

CASSIS
Used in France as an aperitif but elsewhere mainly for mixing. Made from the French black currant.

CHARTREUSE
Secret formula, made by French monks in Tarragona, Spain.

COGNAC
The best of brandy, from France.

COINTREAU
Fine old cognac distilled with orange peel.

CRÈME DE CACAO
Heavy and sweet, made from the beans that supply us with cocoa, distilled with brandy.

CRÈME DE MENTHE
Peppermint liqueur from France and Holland. Three varieties: green, red and white.

CRÈME DE ROSE AND CRÈME DE VIOLETTE
Brandy bases flavoured with essence of the flowers. Left over from the gay nineties, used mainly in pousse-café.

CURAÇAO
Named after the island where the small sweet oranges grow that are used in its composition. Brandy base.

DRAMBUIE
A concentration of venerable Scotch whisky flavoured with honey and herbs.

FIORI D'ALPI
A sweetish liqueur, flavoured with Alpine flowers, featuring a branch of the stem encrusted with sugar in each bottle.

GOLDWASSER

Brandy base flavoured with herbs in which float small specks of gold. Not enough to change the rate of exchange. The old alchemists believed gold was good for internal as well as external disorders.

GRAND MARNIER

A famous version of Curaçao with a secret formula.

GRAPPA

Italian version of marc.

GRENADINE

Made of pomegranates, for flavouring.

KIRSCHWASSER

Distilled from the wild cherries that grow in Switzerland and the Black Forest.

KUMMEL

Especially favoured in the colder countries. Distilled from grain, flavoured with seed of cumin, a plant resembling fennel (Holland).

MARC

Distilled from the grape skins left over from winemaking. Strong.

NOYAU

Made from the crushed seeds of cherries, peaches, plums, apricots on a brandy base.

OXYGENE

Milder absinthe-substitute from Belgium.

PEACH BRANDY

An American product.

PERNOD

Resembling absinthe (from France).

PIMENTO

Made on a Jamaica rum base flavoured with the essence of the pepper. Spicy and hot.

PRUNELLE

Brandy base flavoured with the pits of wild plums. A swell drink for clearing the palate.

STREGA

Similar to Chartreuse and in great favour among Italians.

SUBROUSKA

A green vodka.

SWEDISH PUNCH

A rum derivative liked by the Nordics and sailors. Called Caloric because it gives off heat.

TRIPLE SEC

Curaçao restyled. Colourless, higher-powered, less sweet. One wheel of the Sidecar.

VODKA

An eau de vie from Russia and Poland.

CORDIAL COMBOS

Here are some of the better known methods of gilding the after-dinner lily:

B&B

1 part cognac
1 part Benedictine
Mix, pour into liqueur glass and serve at room temperature.

BRANDY CAMPARELLE

1/4 Curaçao
1/4 yellow Chartreuse
1/4 anisette
1/4 brandy

BROUSSARD'S ORANGE BRULOT

(As served in the famous New Orleans restaurant)

Cut a thin-skinned orange through skin around circumference, careful not to touch the fruit. With a tea-spoon handle, turn the skin back until it forms a cup. Do this on both ends and you have a peeled orange with a cup at each end. Place one cup on your plate. Pour some brandy into upper cup, put a lump of sugar in the brandy, light, stir gently as it burns, then drink it when the flame dies. (Brandy burns more easily if previously warmed; run hot water over the bottle before bringing to table.)

CRÈME DE CACAO, CREAM FLOAT

Gently pour 1 teaspoon heavy cream on to Crème de Cacao in liqueur glass. Serve without stirring, the cream a clean layer on top.

LIZARD SKIN

Hollow out half of a large orange
Pour in large jigger brandy
Light flame, extinguish after a moment, then drink.

POUSSE-CAFÉ

1/6 Maraschino
1/6 raspberry syrup
1/6 Crème de Cacao
1/6 Curaçao
1/6 Chartreuse
1/6 brandy

(The trick is to pour these slowly, one by one, into a liqueur glass so that the colours stay in their strata. This is not governed by law, but specific gravity. You can choose your own colours.) And in the good old summertime, when a ordinary cordial seems forbiddingly heavy, flavour-dravers will favour: Iced Crème de Cage (rich coffee liqueur, one jigger thereof, in glass of shaved ice, filled up with fizz and topped with sweet cream). And Iced Crème de Cacao (voluptuous chocolate liqueur with vanilla aura, similarly coolerized). And short-strawed fragrant verdant Menthe frappe (Crème de Menthe liqueur and shaved-iced in a cocktail glass). And Apricot Delight (1 part each of orange and lemon juices, 2 parts Apricot Brandy, ice-shaken and strained). And Pernod Highball (famous legal version of Absinthe, not made in America, fizzed and cubed).

Highballs

TALL, DARK AND...

The highball, high priest of tall drinks, is nothing but spirits, ice and water or soda, but its concoction is nonetheless governed by basic rules for bringing out the life and flavour to its principal ingredient. Here's how:

1 Use a tall glass – at least 12 oz – preferably uncoloured, definitely sparklingly clean, admirably narrow-mouthed so soda will not collapse ahead of schedule.

2 First put in the ice – one very large or two normal.

3 Next, pour the liquor over the ice. Scotch, bourbon, rye, brandy as you will. The amount varies with customs-of-the-service, but 1½ oz is an average stick.

4 Only then pour in the very cold sparkling water to the desired height – usually four times the amount of liquor. Bubbles thrive on coolness, but rapidly melting ice downs them, so the soda must be pre-chilled in a refrigerator. Some prefer plain water rather than fizz in their highballs, but if you would please palates don't try to pass off the chlorine-clogged stuff that comes from the kitchen faucet. Use an alkaline-sided mineral water, or any purified, bottled aqua – but cold.

5 Spare the spoon and save the drink. The slightest contact with silverware squelches the bubbles – which do the mixing job unassisted. If one of your guests is stir-crazy, give him a plastic or glass swizzle stick.

6 Serve the drink immediately. Recap and replace in the refrigerator any leftover fizz water.

GINGER ALE HIGHBALLS

There's no special name for these whisky-and-ginger ale combinations made by highball rules, except in the case of Scotch which, when coupled with ginger ale, sometimes goes under the heading of 'Presbyterian'.

COLLINS

Sometimes mistakenly labelled John Collins (which is really a gin drink), the whisky Collins goes like this:

Squeeze the juice of a lemon into a tall glass

Add a heaping teaspoon of sugar

Stir, then add 2 ice cubes of plenty of cracked ice

Pour in a generous jigger of whisky – bourbon or rye

Fill with cold soda water

Stir with glass swizzle

It is well to stir before each sip, to keep sugar mixed and drink effervescing. Some garnish with cherry, orange slice.

RICKEY

Put several ice cubes in fizz or highball glass

Squeeze juice of half a lime over ice, then drop lime skin into glass

Pour in 1 jigger whisky

Fill with seltzer

Stir with glass rod

WHISKY SHAKE

Juice of 2 limes

½ teaspoon sugar

2 oz Whisky

Shake with great quantities of fine ice; strain into tall flute glass.

MISSISSIPPI PUNCH

Stir in Collins glass:

2 dashes lemon juice

1 teaspoon sugar

2 dashes Angostura bitters

Add:

1 oz Whisky

1 ½ oz Rum

1 oz Brandy

Fill with cracked ice; garnish with fruit if desired; attack with straws.

HORSE'S NECK

Strictly speaking, this is a teetotaller's drink, but add whisky to the basic and see how it goes:

Peel the whole rind of a lemon

Place it in a Collins glass, spiralling up from bottom and hooking over edge

Add 2 cubes of ice

Pour in 1 jigger whisky

Fill with cold ginger ale

A dash of bitters is sometimes added to the whisky.

MAMIE TAYLOR

Squeeze ½ lime into Collins glass

Add 2 cubes of ice

Pour in 1 jigger Scotch

Fill with cold ginger ale

MILK PUNCH

Into shaker filled with shaved ice put:

1 teaspoon sugar

1 jigger whisky

Fill glass with milk. Shake. Strain into large goblet or highball glass. Sprinkle with nutmeg.

MINT JULEP

Creeping gingerly onto the julep battleground, armed with enough formulae to please all violent schools of thought on the subject of creating this classic among long drinks, Esquire takes sides only to the extent of backing these general rules;

1 Use a prechilled, dry 12 or 14 oz glass, tall and slim, if the traditional silver beaker is not available.

2 Crush the ice by putting it in a bag or towel, then hammering it with mallet or banging it against a sturdy sink. Then be sure it is absolutely dry, draining off the water, before putting it in the glass.

3 Use only the freshest mint and, of that, the smallest, most tender leaves.

4 Don't handle the glass with bare hands. Use a cloth, or serve with a doily, if you would preserve the frost.

5 The glass will not frost if in the wind, if wet, with undried ice or if excessively handled. You can sometimes speed the frost by twirling the glass or by placing in coldest part of refrigerator for about 30 minutes.

Here, then, is an assortment of recipes:

JULEP

Use a 14 oz or 16 oz silver julep cup. Dissolve a half or one lump of granulated sugar in clear spring water. Add two or three sprigs of tender mint, place gently (don't bruise the mint). Fill the cup with cracked ice and add 2 full jiggers of Kentucky bourbon whisky. Stir gently and refill the julep cup with cracked ice. Take a full bunch of tender mint, cutting the ends to bleed, and place on top. Let it stand for about five minutes before serving. There should be a small linen doily with each julep, as the frost on the cups make it uncomfortable to hold.

VIRGINIA JULEP

(A test of patience!)

Pour a measure of bourbon over several sprigs of mint and allow this to stand for half an hour.

Dissolve a teaspoon of sugar in a little water and place in a glass. When half an hour has passed, remove the mint from the whisky and pour the bourbon into the sugar and water. Pour this mixture back and forth between the two glasses until the liquids are well mixed, then...

Fill a glass with finely crushed ice and pour the mixture over it. Stir briskly until the frost forms on the glass, then fill to the top of the glass with sprigs of fresh mint.

GIN

GIN AND TONIC

1 generous jigger of gin
One-quarter fresh lime
1 split of tonic water

Serve in regular highball glass with cube of ice.

FRENCH '75'

2 oz of gin
1 teaspoon powdered sugar
Juice of one fresh lime or one-fourth lemon

Shake well with ice. Pour into ten-ounce glass, and then fill with champagne. Some add 5 dashes of bitters.

GIN CUP

Take a pint cup, pure silver
Fill it with crushed ice
Put in juice one-half lemon
Put in tablespoonful powdered sugar
Joggle cup *slightly* for five minutes
Add large jigger best gin
Let stand until entire outside heavily frosted

Sip quietly:
only a mutt will talk or read
After 15 minutes of sedate joy
Take 15 minutes more of same
The day becomes beautiful!

GIN JULEP

Bruise four sprigs of mint with a spoonful of powdered sugar. Add two ounces of gin. Fill tall glass with crushed ice and stir until frosted.

GIN RICKEY

(Dry or Sloe)

Squeeze half a lime into ordinary bar glass, over cubes of ice. Toss in limeskin, add 1 jigger of gin and fill with soda water. Stir briefly. (Dash of Grenadine sometimes added). For a sweeter drink, when dry gin is used, crush the lime-half with 1 teaspoon sugar before adding ice, gin and sparkly.

LEE MILLER'S FROBISHER

Use 10 oz glass
2 oz Gin
1 dash bitters
1 lemon peel
Plenty cracked ice

Fill glass to brim with champagne Stir.

SINGAPORE SLING

1 jigger sloe gin
½ jigger dry gin
½ jigger apricot brandy
½ jigger cherry brandy
½ lime juice
1 teaspoon sugar

Stir in 12 oz glass with cracked ice. Fill with seltzer water. Decorate with cherry, slice of orange and stick of fresh pineapple. (Drink will be a deep red in colour.)

TOM COLLINS

Squeeze the juice of a lemon in a tall glass, add a heaping teaspoon of sugar, a generous jigger of Tom or London gin, plenty of cracked ice, and fill with soda water. It is well to stir before each gulp, as that keeps the sugar mixed and the drink effervescing. Variation: add several lusty shots of Angostura bitters.

RUM

BACARDI COLLINS

Mix in shaker:

Juice of one lime

1 teaspoon sugar

1 jigger Bacardi

Shake well with ice; strain into Collins glass ballasted with ice cubes. Fill with fizz.

COCONUT COOLER

Get a coconut; bore out one of the eyes and drain off the milk. Mix half milk and half Jamaica rum, ice, and fill with charged water.

CUBA LIBRE

Into Collins glass squeeze one-half lime, then drop in the skin. Add cubes of ice, the pour in:

2 oz Puerto Rican or Cuban rum

Fill with cold Coca-Cola

Serve with a stirring rod.

CUBAN COOLER

Ice cubes in tall glass – measure of favourite rum – fill with ginger ale – decorate with sprig of mint.

MILK PUNCH

(As served on rolling days at sea and a rainy day in Colon, Panama.)

1 teaspoon of sugar

2 pieces of ice

½ cocktail glass of rum (or brandy or whisky)

Put in shaker and fill with rich milk. Shake well and serve with nutmeg on top.

PLANTERS PUNCH

There are almost as many version of this tall cooler as there are planters, but the 1-2-3's go something like this:

One of sour (juice of one lime)

Two of sweet (two teaspoons sugar)

Three of strong (3 oz redolent old heavy-bodied Jamaica rum)

Four of weak (ice and water)

Lots of shaking and what garnishment you please.

Or this, for the less sugar-sold:

One of Sweet (1 dessert spoon sugar or gum syrup)

Two of sour (2 dessert spoons fresh lime or lemon juice)

Three of weak (3 tablespoons fine ice)

Four of strong (4 tablespoons rum)

At the conclusion of this aria, add Angostura dashes; stir or shake and strain into tall glass of cracked ice fancied up with ½ slice lemon, ½ slice orange, sliver of pineapple, Maraschino cherry and anything else you may care to contribute. Trinidad's prideful prescription uses a teaspoon of Angostura, is garnished solely with a slice of lemon and is sprinkled with nutmeg.

RUM COLLINS

Juice of 1 lime of one-half lemon

1 teaspoon sugar

2 oz rum

Shake with ice, pour unstrained into Collins glass and fill with sparkling water. Or mix juice and sugar in bottom of glass, add ice cubes, then pour in rum and seltzer. Bottled Collins mix can be used: ice cubes, then rum, then bottled mix. Deluxe version: use 1 tablespoon Falernum in place of sugar. Variation: add a dash of Angostura bitters.

BRANDY

BRANDY FIZZ

Juice of one lemon

1 bar spoon sugar

1 jigger brandy

2 dashes yellow Chartreuse

Shake well with ice; strain; fill glass with siphon.

BRANDY FIX

Dissolve one teaspoon of sugar in one teaspoon of water in small tumbler. Add juice of half a lemon, 1 jigger of brandy, ½ jigger cherry brandy, fill the glass with chipped ice, stir and serve with a straw.

BRANDY MINT JULEP

3 jiggers cognac brandy

4 sprigs mint (uncrushed)

1 teaspoonful powdered sugar

Place mint in large glass, and then dissolve sugar. Add brandy and shaved ice. Stir well till very cold.

BRANDY PUNCH

Fill wineglass half full shaved ice

Add one teaspoon sugar

1 teaspoon pineapple juice

Juice of one-fourth of a lemon

A few dashes of lime juice

1 large jigger brandy

Stir well, add a squirt of soda, serve with a dash of rum and fruit on top.

EGG LEMONADE

Fill your shaker half full with chopped ice, add one fresh egg, one teaspoon sugar, juice of one lemon, one jigger of brandy. Shake well, strain into large glass and fill with soda.

FRENCH '75' OR KING'S PEG

Juice of one lemon

1 teaspoon fine granulated sugar

2 oz brandy

5 dashes bitters

Shake with cracked ice and pour unstrained into highball glass. Fill with champagne and stir gently.

SANGRIA (ARGENTINEAN)

Proportions for this brandy julep vary, so follow the general julep rules and follow your taste with these ingredients:

brandy

claret

orange juice

Triple Sec

WHITEHALL PUNCH
(Holiday Drink)
Created by Florida-promoter
Henry M. Flagler

Into a mixing glass squeeze the juice of 1 lime. Add 1 jigger brandy, 1 bar spoon Grenadine, 1 dash syrup. Fill with cracked ice and shake well. Then strain into a tall glass which has been well frosted and is full of snow ice. After straining the drink into the glass, fill up with more snow ice and top off with seltzer. (For the full treatment, you would place glass in individual silver bowl and pack shaved ice to within 1 inch of brim.) Decorate with a strawberry, slice of orange and pineapple. Serve 2 straws and sip slowly to savour delicate bouquet.

CLARET LEMONADE

Fill a tall glass ¾ full of lemonade prepared in the usual manner. Atop this pour claret – carefully – so that it remains on top. When the partaker inserts spoon and stirs, it's a pretty sight.

EMPIRE PUNCH

(As served at Casino Bar, Dieppe)

In a large tumbler put three or four lumps of ice, then add:

1 teaspoon Curaçao

1 teaspoon Benedictine

1 teaspoon brandy

1 wineglass of claret

Fill to top of glass with champagne, stir well, decorate with fruits.

PORT WINE SANGAREE

1 bar spoon sugar

1 jigger water

4 oz port wine

Mix in bottom of tall glass, add ice, then fill with seltzer.

RHINE WINE AND SPRITZER

This is ½ Rhine wine, ½ seltzer water in tall glass with 2 or 3 ice-cubes – a perfect drink for the very young or the very cautious.

(Variations: Add 1 jigger dry sherry ...add 1 tablespoon lemon juice... garnish with cucumber slice.)

ROYAL PLUSH

Into a tall glass with ice cubes, pour ½ burgundy, ½ champagne. Stir gently.

SAUTERNES CUP

When there's a group thirst to be quenched of an afternoon, put big lumps ice in a glass pitcher, pour in:

1 quart sauternes

1 pint soda

1 wineglass sherry

1 pony brandy

Add:

Rind of one lemon

3 slices orange

3 slices lemon

1 slice cucumber peel

Any fresh berries available

Stir and serve in tall glasses ornamented with fruit. Or substitute champagne for sauternes, add 1 pony white Curaçao and use fresh mint instead of fruit.

SIR CHARLES PUNCH

(Christmas)

Fill a large tumbler half full with shave ice. Add to this one teaspoon of granulate sugar, one wineglass of port, ½ glass of brandy, ½ glass of Curaçao. Stir well with a spoon. Ornament the top with slices of orange, pineapple and split grapes.

WINE COLLINS

Squeeze juice of ½ lemon into Collins glass, fill to half-way mark with any table-wine. Add ice cubes, fill with sparkling water and stir. Sugar may be added to lemon juice if desired.

Beer

THE COOLER WITH THE COLLAR

There's not much you can 'do' with beer, except indulge in the pleasant task of drinking it. But in the interests of justice to the cooler with the collar, Esquire offers this 10-plank platform for handling foam on the range.

1 Bottled beer doesn't thrive on sunlight. Hide it away till you are ready to put it away.
2 Don't keep it in a warm place, either.
3 Nor up against the ice, nor cube compartment, in your refrigerator. It needs coolness, not such extreme cold as to cloud it.
4 If cloudy, remove from excessive chill which has causes this temporary condition. Served immediately, it would have a weak head.
5 No jiggling or bouncing before serving.
6 Pry off bottle caps briskly, and plunge can opener boldly, avoid spraying.
7 When pouring, tilt glass so that beer makes its entrée on the slant; then straighten for a collar.
8 Glasses should be washed in a solution of salt or soda. Never soap. And do not dry with a cloth.
9 Ale and pewter are particularly congenial.
10 Steins with hinged lids keep beer fresh for leisurely drinkers.

And here are three old-time combinations to vary your pursuit of happiness:

PORTER

(Named for porters who in the 16th to 18th century went after the stuff when the master was abed.)

1 1 part ale
2 1 part beer
3 1 part two-penny (a milder beer)

'ARF AND 'ARF

1 part ale
1 part beer

HUCKLE-MY-BUTT

1 quart beer
½ pint of brandy
2 eggs
Sugar to taste
Small amounts of cinnamon, cloves and nutmeg

Stir thoroughly until well mixed.

Punches

TO BOWL YOU OVER

PUNCHES – COLD

Bearing no resemblance to the sloppy 'pink lemonade pond' that functions, amid dirty glasses and wet tablecloth, at nondescript dances where the budget for 'refreshments' is modest to the point of prudery – these are punches with punch. An honest bowl of cheer is a natural hub of a party, and though you'd best have a Scotch-and-soda bar for die-hards who regard a punch bowl as a quaint curio, you'll be surprised at the converts you win with some of these mixtures. Delmonico glasses or outright tumblers rather than those cute-handled cuppies known as knuckle-traps.

ARISTOCRAT SPARKLING PUNCH

1 bottle burgundy
4 ounces brandy
1 quart sparkling water
2 bottles champagne
1 cup cube sugar

Dissolve sugar in a cup of sparkling water and pour into punch bowl. Add burgundy and brandy, stirring well. Place block of ice in bowl, and add champagne and the balance of sparkling water. Garnish top of ice block with strawberries or raspberries, or other fruit in season, and float thin slices of two oranges on top of punch.

BRANDY PUNCH

Juice two oranges
Juice six lemons
4 oz powdered sugar
½ pint Curaçao
1 quart brandy
Spoonful Grenadine

Pour into punch bowl over a large piece of ice. Add 1 bottle soda water.

STRAWBERRY BOWLE

Place in a bowl one quart of washed and hulled strawberries. (Use wild strawberries, if possible.) Cover with 1 cup sugar and 1 cup cognac. Shake bowl slightly to mix ingredients and put in icebox to stand about eight hours. When ready serve, add three bottles of well-iced Moselle or Rhine wine. Do not add ice.

CHAMPAGNE PUNCH

To each bottle of champagne add one bottle of club soda, one pony of brandy, one pony of Triple Sec liqueur; the rind of one orange, cut very thin. Little or no powdered sugar. And no lemon. Deposit berg of ice.

Decorate with sliced fresh pineapple and orange, and plenty of fresh mint. Crusted fresh strawberries add a gala touch to looks and flavour.

Variation: Cointreau instead of Triple Sec.

CHAMPAGNE CUP

Carve and shave a piece of ice 8 inches long so it will stand in a pitcher and leave 1½ inch space all around. In this space place 3 round slices of orange, 3 round slices of pineapple, and preserved cherries in between. Three long slices of fresh cucumber rind are next put in place. Now add 1 bottle of champagne, and 2 ponies each of brandy and Benedictine, and stir. Fresh mint is used as top decoration.

CHRISTMAS RUM PUNCH
(Cold)

Juice of four oranges
Juice of two lemons
Diced pineapple
2 oz granulated sugar
1 pony Curaçao
1 small bottle Maraschino cherries
1 bottle old Jamaica or New England rum
1 bottle club soda

Place in punch bowl fruit juices, cherries and liquid of cherries; add garnishment consisting of 1 orange thinly sliced and 2 lemons ditto, and the diced pineapple. Also the sugar, Curaçao and rum. Let stand for 2 hours. When due to be served, add ice (chunk) and club soda.

CLARET OR BURGUNDY CUP

To each bottle of claret or burgundy add one bottle of club soda, one glass of sherry, one pony of Triple Sec and one pony of brandy; also the rind of one lemon cut very thin; powdered sugar to taste.

Decorate with fresh pineapple, orange, and one slice of fresh cucumber rind. Let brew a short time before serving, then add a boulder of ice and, if available, a flock of fresh mint. Fresh (or frosted -packed) raspberries and peaches are appropriate dunnage.

COLD APPLE TODDY

Roast 1 dozen apples with their skins on. Mash while hot. Add 1 lb. sugar and 2 quarts of boiling water. Then 1 quart apple brandy and 1 pint peach brandy. Cover so as not to squander aroma. And don't go sniffing at it.

When cool, strain coarsely, permitting pulp to come through. Add 1 pint sherry. Bowl with ice.

FLORIDA PUNCH

1 oz grapefruit juice
1 oz orange juice
1 oz heavy rum
½ oz brandy

Shake and strain into tall glass filled with cracked ice.

FRUIT CUP

Take whatever fruit you have on hand in season, such as peaches, strawberries, plums, raspberries. Wash the fruit, slice, put in a bowl with half a cup of sugar and one cup of brandy, rye or rum. Let it stand over night and when ready to use pour into a gallon of chilled Chablis, Pouilly Fuisse or the best dry domestic white wine available. Variations: Use 1 cup sugar...add a quart of sparkling water and a glass of gin. The top of the bowl may be dressed with the fruits of the season.

GIN BOWL

1 gallon dry white wine
1 bottle of gin
1 cup of green tea
3 lemons sliced

This can be stepped up considerably by the addition of one cup of heavy rum or brandy.

ORANGE CUP

(For 12 people)

Juice of six oranges
2 pints carbonated water
Sweeten with sugar and put in punch
 bowl with
16 ounces of rum
2 ounces of Curaçao
Iceberg

PICNIC PUNCH

(Ideal for washtub and cake of ice)

1 pineapple, cut up
12 lemons, cut up
1 gallon gin
2 gallons white wine
1 pint of rum

Makes 30 picnickers very happy.

RED WINE CUP

1 bottle of claret or burgundy
1 bottle of club soda
1 wine glass of sherry
1 pony Curaçao
1 pony brandy
Rind of 1 lemon, cut very thin
Smidgen of powdered sugar

Adorn with fresh pineapple, orange, fresh mint and slice of fresh cucumber rind. Let stand an hour or so for interjubilation of ingredients. Add large berg of ice when ready to serve.

RUM PUNCH

Into a bowl put 2 oz granulated sugar and juice of 4 large grapefruit. Stir to dissolve the sugar and add 1 bottle of rum, 4 oz brandy and 4 oz of Benedictine, 2 teaspoons of bitters, and the juice of 1 lime. Stir well and add ½ nutmeg grated and the peeling of 1 lime.

SAUTERNES PUNCH

Slice some peaches and apricots (twice as many of the former), add a little brandy, cover with sugar and let stand for a few hours. When ready to serve, put the mixture in a bowl or pitcher and pour over it chilled sauternes and charged water. Ice slightly so as not to weaken the drink.

WHITE WINE CUP

1 bottle of white burgundy or dryish Graves, 1 bottle of club soda, 1 wine glass of sherry, a pony apiece of anisette and brandy; rind of 1 lemon; powdered sugar in moderation; thin slices of fresh pineapple; mint; ice.

PUNCHES - HOT

In most cases these warmers of the inner man can be made by the mug in the same proportions as those given for group gurgling, but where such perennial favourites as hot buttered rum and hot milk punch are involved, we've given both 'bowl' and individual recipes.

ALE FLIP

Beat separately 2 egg whites and 4 yolks. Combine them, adding 4 tablespoons of moistened sugar, and ½ nutmeg grated.

Put 1 quart ale in saucepan and bring to boil. Pour into it the egg-sugar mixture, gradually, stirring as you add. Transfer the steaming result to robust pitcher and pour back and forth rapidly between this pitcher and its twin brother, each time holding the pourer high above the receiver, till a handsome froth is attained.

Serve in mugs or large goblets. One pillow to every customer.

ARCHBISHOP PUNCH

Stick cloves into a good-sized orange and toast it in a warm oven. When the skin is brown, cut into quarters, seed, put into a saucepan and cover with a bottle of claret. Add sugar and let it simmer until hot.

BISHOP

Stick an orange full of cloves and roast it in front of the Yule log (or in the oven) until soft and brownish; cut it in quarters, pour over it a quart of hot port wine, and let simmer for half an hour. Serve in punch glasses. The aroma is almost as good as the flavour.

BLACK STRIPE

*(Served anywhere
in the tropics)*

1 tablespoon of honey dissolved in
    hot water

½ cocktail glass of old rum

Fill glass with hot water, grate nutmeg on top.

BLUE BLAZER

1 jigger Scotch or rye

1 lump sugar

Very hot water

Set liquid on fire and pour from one
    glass to another

Twist of lemon peel on top

BRANDY PUNCH

Take the peel of two lemons, a pinch of cinnamon and a bit of nutmeg, mace and cloves. Add this to three quarters pound of sugar and a half pint of boiling water. Let it simmer on the fire and then strain. Now add a bottle of brandy and the juice of two lemons. Added effect is gained by setting on fire before serving.

CAFÉ GROG

Mix a pony of Jamaica or Bacardi rum, two lumps of sugar, a slice of lemon, a spoonful of brandy and a demitasse of black coffee. Heat and serve hot.

CHRISTMAS RUM PUNCH

(Hot)

6 oranges

½ gallon sweet cider

1 bottle Jamaica rum, bestest

Sugar to taste

Whole cloves

Ground cinnamon and nutmeg

Stick the oranges full of cloves and bake them in the oven until they soften. Place oranges in the punch bowl, pour over them the rum and granulated sugar to taste. Set fire to rum and in a few minutes add the cider slowly to extinguish the flame. Stir in cinnamon and nutmeg, and keep the mixture hot.

EGGNOG

(For Solo Drinking)

Open fresh egg into large glass. Add two teaspoonfuls powdered sugar. Add small amount of milk and fill glass with very hot rum. Mix well and add dash Angostura bitters.

ENGLISH
CHRISTMAS PUNCH

Take two bottles of good red wine, add one quart of strong tea, and the juice of one lemon and one orange. Heat thoroughly and just before serving, supporting on irons across the bowl two pounds of sugar soaked in rum. Light the rum and as the flame dies add the rest of the bottle of rum.

FLAMES OVER JERSEY

1 quart apple brandy

1 cup sugar

1 oz to 1 jigger Angostura bitters

Lemon peels, to taste

Set afire and stir, with blue flames flickering (lights more easily if warmed first). Then douse flames with 1 quart boiling water, stir and serve pronto in glass or silver mugware.

GLUEHWEIN

Boil in an earthen jug one glass of good claret or burgundy. (Never use a fortified wine.) In the pot put about 3 inches of sugar, 1 slice of orange peel and 1 slice of lemon peel. If a quantity is made it is better, allowing the earthen jug to stand on a slow fire and brought to near boiling point slowly.

GUARDSMAN'S PUNCH

(For six or so)

1 ounce of port wine
1 pint of fresh green tea
4 ounces of sugar
Peel of one lemon
1 glass of brandy
1 bottle of Scotch whisky

Heat and serve piping hot.

HOT BUTTERED RUM

Dissolve 1 or 2 lumps of sugar in a little hot water, add a wineglass of rum, a piece of butter the size of a small walnut, and fill the mug or glass with hot water. Sprinkle nutmeg on top. (A teaspoon of spices such as cinnamon and cloves may be added to this mixture, or you might garnish with clovestudded lemon.)

HOT BUTTERED TODDY

Bestow in deserving mug:

1 hooker doggonedest best whisky
1 ounce orange juice
1 teaspoonful sugar

Fill up with hot water. Stir inhalingly. Add about a quarter of a pat of butter as a floater on top.

HOT LOCOMOTIVE

1 yolk egg
½ tablespoon sugar
1 pony honey

Stir these well with a spoon.
Add:

½ pony Curaçao
1½ wineglass burgundy or claret

Place over heat until boiling. Pour

from cooking dish to mug several times. Add slice lemon and little cinnamon.

HOT MILK PUNCH

1 tablespoon sugar
¼ wineglass rum
¾ wineglass brandy

Stir in large glass and fill with hot milk. Add nutmeg.

HOT MINT BURGUNDY DELIGHT

6 fresh crisp mint leaves
1 piece lemon peel
1 tablespoon sugar
3 oz (or 3 tablespoons) burgundy

Muddle well together and add a few drops of Maraschino cherry juice syrup, one small stick of cinnamon and two whole cloves. Then add 3 oz or 3 tablespoons of burgundy and an equal amount of hot water. Stir and serve.

HOT IRISH PUNCH

Dissolve 3 lumps of sugar in a little hot water in a large glass. Add small amount of lemon juice, and one wine glass Irish whisky. Fill glass with hot water and stir well. Add nutmeg and slice of lemon.

HOT RUM PUNCH

1 pt. Puerto Rico rum
½ pt. cognac
½ wineglass Kummel
½ wineglass Benedictine
1 lemon or lime peel
1 orange peel
1 sliced orange or grapefruit
1 sliced lemon or lime
Sugar to taste

Put all in bowl, add 3 pts. boiling water. Stir well and serve.

HOT TODDY

(Bowl)

1 quart rye, bourbon, Scotch, apple
    brandy or grape brandy

2 quarts boiling water

Clove-studded lemon slices

Bits of stick cinnamon

Sugar to taste

Pour boiling water over spiced and sugared liquor, stir then serve steaming hot with one of the lemon slices in each drink.

HOT TODDY

(Individual)

Mix double-shot of favourite whisky or brandy with 1 teaspoon (or less) sugar. Fill glass with hot water and garnish with clove-studded lemon slice and bits of stick cinnamon.

HOT WINE PUNCH

Boil three spoonfuls of sugar in a half pint of water, add six cloves, three small pieces of stick cinnamon, rind of whole lemon cut very thin. When this comes to a boil, add one bottle of good claret or burgundy and serve piping hot.

HOT SPICED WINE

Put a bottle of good American burgundy or claret, without uncorking, into a deep pot of water on the stove. Let it heat up, but don't let it actually boil, rescuing bottle when on the verge. Uncork and pour into preheated pitcher. Add hot syrup made with sugar and water, spiced as desired. Toss in sliced (or halved) lemons and oranges and any other flavourable cargo that occurs to you. Serve in glass mugs with a stick of cinnamon in each.

In instances where more intensive grape glow is required, a bottle of brandy is substituted for the wine, with 1½ quarts of water as dilutor. Where party opinion is stalemated on the question of Wine vs. Brandy, the solution is Hot Wine with Brandy – the brandy inserted to the extent of 3 ponies per bottle of wine; spices and decor same as in Hot Spiced Wine. The only hard and fast rule is: Never let the wine or spirits boil.

LAMB'S WOOL

(A corruption of 'al maes abhal' ancient term for a harvest holiday, November)

Put six baked apples in a large dish. Cut or break apples so that their pulp is exposed. Pour over these one quart of hot ale. Sugar to taste and add ginger and nutmeg in small quantities.

MULLED WINE

1 pint Burgundy or Claret, and extra
    glass of same

½ nutmeg

Sugar to taste

Yolks of 4 eggs

Grate nutmeg into pint of wine; sweeten to taste. Place on fire and bring to boil, then set aside for a moment. Beat and strain the egg-yolks, adding to them the glass of cold wine; then mix the result gradually with the hot spiced wine and pour back and forth half a dozen times.

Put total mixture on the fire and heat slowly till piping and thick. Ladle it up and down.

Serve in mugs with laths of toast on the side.

MULLED ALE

Heat an iron poker till red-hot; immerse it slowly in a mug (preferably pewter) of ale, taking care not to cause an overflow.

NEGRITA GROG

¼ brandy

¼ rum

¼ sugar

¼ strong tea

Add a small glass Curaçao, mix well, then pour into a large glass until it is half full. Fill the glass with hot water, slice of lemon on top.

NEGUS

Pour a pint of port wine into a bowl and add ten lumps of sugar that have been rubbed on a lemon rind. Add the juice of one lemon. A small pinch of nutmeg. Now add a quart of boiling water and serve while hot.

NIGHT CAP

Beat up a yolk of a fresh egg, add pony of anisette, one pony orange Curaçao, one pony of brandy. Add hot water and leave a call for 2 o'clock.

OLD CASTLE PUNCH

Take a granite saucepan and melt two pounds of loaf sugar in one quart of water, letting the mixture come to the boil. Now reduce the heat under the pan and add two bottles of Rhine wine, not permitting the mixture to boil. Soak a lump of sugar in a silver spoon and set it afire, holding it over the pan. Pour gradually over the sugar a pint of good rum. Serve very hot as it comes off the fire.

REGENT'S PUNCH

Take two glasses of white wine and add one glass of Madeira and a half glass of rum. Mix this with one pint of very hot tea.

RUM FLIP

(For British Sailors)

1 egg

½ tablespoon powdered sugar

1 glass of rum, brandy, port wine, sherry or whisky

Heat well, stirring constantly.

SACK POSSET

(A Two-Pot Circus)

Introduce to each other in a saucepan:

½ pint sherry (not 'cooking' sherry)

½ pint ale

Slowly bring to a boil.

Meanwhile, in another saucepan, similarly heat up a quart of milk.

Pour the boiling mix gradually into the sherry and ale. Sweeten to taste. Add grated nutmeg.

Transfer to preheated dish or jug, equipped with a cover, and stand near fire for two or three hours. Quaff in mugs.

SANO GROG

Into a highball glass, put a teaspoonful of powdered sugar, a pony of whisky, a pony of Curaçao, a pony of Jamaica or Bacardi rum. Add three times the quantity of boiling water. Serve with a slice of lemon on top.

SKI JUMPER'S THÉ DANSANT

1 pint strong hot green tea

Juice of 4 lemons and 6 oranges

8 oz granulated sugar, stirred till dissolved

1 wineglass Curaçao or Triple Sec

1 bottle rum, heated

Serve hot and watch your slaloms.

SKIPPER'S PARTICULAR

1 pint Jamaica rum

½ pint cognac

2 oz Kummel

2 oz Benedictine

Rind of 1 lemon

Ditto of 1 orange

3 pints of piping hot water

Sugar as you please

SOLDIER'S CAMPING PUNCH

1 large kettle boiled strong coffee

4 pounds lump sugar

4 bottles brandy

2 bottles Jamaica rum

Pour brandy and rum over sugar and place over fire until sugar is dissolved. Add to coffee mixture and stir well.

SUN VALLEY

Heat a quart of thick cream almost to the boiling point, add two tablespoons of powdered sugar. Beat the yolks of four fresh eggs with a little milk and add this to the cream. Now add a large glass of rum (Jamaica type) and stir thoroughly. Serve in cups.

TOM AND JERRY

Take as many eggs as persons served. Beat up the whites and yolks separately. Add one teaspoonful of granulated sugar for each egg and mix whites with yolks. When ready to serve, take two tablespoons of this batter and put in a large mug or tumbler. Now add one pony of brandy and one pony of Jamaica rum, stirring constantly to avoid

curdling. Fill to the top with hot water or hot milk and stir until smooth. Usually a little grated nutmeg is sprinkled on top.

(NOTE: Some, finding water too thin and milk too rich and filling, use half hot milk, half boiling water. Vary the proportions of rum or brandy, emphasising one or the other, or try it with bourbon and brandy, bourbon alone or bourbon and rum.)

WHISKY PUNCH

One pint of whisky and two glasses of brandy are mixed with the juice and peel of one lemon. Then add one wineglass of boiling ale. Stir in one-half pound of powdered sugar and a quart of boiling water.

ZERO NIGHT PUNCH

(Six to eight persons)

½ cup of granulated sugar

1 quart of milk

2 whole lemon peels, pared very thin

Place in double boiler, and let come to a boil. Infuse 5 or 6 teabags for 1 or 1½ minutes. Remove bags and add 10oz of apple brandy. Boil for 2 or 3 minutes, and serve very hot with a little nutmeg on top.

WASSAIL BOWL

Put one pound of sugar in a bowl and over this pour three quarts of beer and four glasses of sherry. Add small amount of nutmeg and ginger and float a sliced lemon on top.

Egg-Nog

SEASONED TIPPLING

To tradition-steeped Christmas celebrants, the season would be bleak unless thickly upholstered with Eggnog. Basically eggs, sugar, liquors, milk and cream, served very cold in glass cups, the eggnog is sometimes underpinned with rye or bourbon, sometimes with brandy and rum. Try these, mixing up 2-egg batches until your experiments have convinced you of the best method:

VIRGINIA EGGNOG

One dozen eggs of the freshest. Separate. Put whites aside for the moment. Beat yolks strenuously. While still breathing, slowly add 12 tablespoons of granulated sugar and continue *à tempo* until sugar is entirely dissolved. Slowly pour in 1 generous pint cognac, still stirring the while. Follow with 1/2 pint (on the slim side) *full bodied rum*. (The completed concoction should not taste of rum-in-the-nude. In other words, the rum must not boss the mixture. If it is very pungent, pull down the rum content and increase the *cognac*. In any case, the quality of the cognac will determine the character of the brew. So have your cognac good!) Pouring the liquor into the yolks has the effect of cooking them more lovingly than any stove could. Now take 1 pint milk and 1/2 pint heavy cream. (Cream may be whipped, but this makes the result a bit rich, so to some tastes plain cream is preferable.) Stir in milk and cream. Clean off egg beating equipment and go at the whites till they will stand without hitching. Fold the whites into the general mixture. Then stir in 1 grated nutmeg. If outcome is too sweet to suit taste, extra brandy may now be added till it fits. Will serve 10 to 12 people. For open-house purposes, you would need double, triple, or quadruple this amount. For convenience's sake, some people make this eggnog the day before the party and put it in the refrigerator till wanted. Parked there – or even on the pantry window sill – it will keep perfectly for several days if air-tight glass jars are used.

BALTIMORE EGGNOG

Take six eggs. Beat the yolks and whites separately. Beat until very light. Add $1/4$ pound of sugar to whites and $1/4$ pound of sugar to yolks. Beat again. Stir into the yolks one quart of rich milk and one quart of rich cream. Then stir in very slowly $3/4$ pint of *Old New England rum*, or *Jamaica rum* (a good heavy rum is best) and $3/4$ pint of good brandy. Whisky may be used if desired, but real Maryland eggnog never has whisky in it. Add $1/2$ grated nutmeg and about two dozen whole cloves. Let stand in the refrigerator for about four hours before serving. When ready to serve, shake well to mix the milk and cream, which have a habit of separating.

AND STILL ANOTHER

(This one with Bourbon)

1 doz fresh eggs

1 doz tablespoons granulated sugar

1 pint best bourbon whisky

1 pint heavy-bodied bouquet rum

1 wineglass peach cordial

1 quart milk

1 quart cream

Grated nutmeg

Segregate egg yolks, beat them and add to them the sugar, working it in gradually; then half of the milk. Still stirring, insert the whisky and the rum. Let stand 15 minutes or so to give these elements a chance to get well acquainted; then add the other half of the milk, and also the cream, likewise the peach cordial. The whites of the eggs which have undergone a separate lashing until stiff, are now neatly folded into the mixture, which gets a light shower of nutmeg as a send-off.

OLD VIRGINIA EGGNOG

(Thick)

12 eggs, new born

10 oz granulated sugar

1 quart finest brandy

1 pint Jamaica rum, rich and ripe

1 gallon heavy cream

Beat the 12 yolks relentlessly, adding the granulated sugar, then alternate shots of the brandy and rum till full amounts are incorporated. Then three-fourths of the heavy cream and, foldingly half of the egg whites, prebeaten in a side dish. Whereupon, beat up other half of egg whites stiffer than stiff, adding to them the cup of powdered s ugar, plus (lightly stirred in) the other quart of cream, and fold this side show into the main show. Twelve hours' rest in a cool place of safety will be beneficial. Partakers will need spoons as this calls for spadework.

FROZEN EGGNOG

(As served in New York's Algonquin)

12 egg yolks

1 pound sugar

1 gallon cream, whipped

1 pint brandy

1 pint Jamaica rum

Beat the egg yolks very light and add the sugar, then the whipped cream. Freeze till firm. Then add the brandy and rum and turn freezer rapidly a few times to mix well. Eat with holiday cake. Serves 24.

Pick-me-ups

FOR SLOWER LET-YOU-DOWNS

The only thing more horrible than a really first-rate hangover – one with long, matted hair and a guttural voice – is the hangover remedy which well-meaning friends force down your gullet the morning after. Although the medical profession in general seems to take the attitude that you've made your own hangover so you're welcome to groan in it, one heroic group of physicians has come up with these pointers:

1 Much of your morning-after misery is due to the anaesthetising after-effects of ethyl alcohol; you and your organs are still partially paralysed. Your sleeping stomach should be given TIME to get back in working condition before you throw ice-water, coffee, Hair of the Dog or *anything* into it. Thus, the best thing to 'take' for a hangover is NOTHING.

2 Though your tongue is parched and your mouth tastes as if you have

been sitting up all night licking Lithuanian postage stamps, don't bolt down large quantities of ice-water. Sip *warm* water – *slowly*.

3 Upon arising, try to force yourself to do a little mild exercising – or, if that seems impossible, stand at the open window and breathe deeply as many times as you can stand it. An oxygen tent is the one real aid to a hangover, but since so few homes are equipped with oxygen tents these days deep breathing will serve as a substitute.

4 Only when you begin to feel actually hungry, meaning that your gastric juices are beginning to function again, it is safe to take an alkalising salt or a laxative.

5 And *then* what you need is a pick-me-up composed of (1) something to give your stomach a kick in the pants and (2) something easily digestible for nourishment. No. 1 is the reason why so many 'remedies' contain Tabasco, bitters or absinthe. No. 2 explains raw eggs, the most digestible food on the market. Since The Hair of the Dog courts alcoholism, we recommend the non-alcoholic Prairie Oyster school, or the mild beer varieties of 'cures'. But inasmuch as all this requires a great deal of willpower and is largely a matter of conjecture anyway, the following list includes more potent pick-ups.

Incidentally, prevention is always more successful than cure. Short of sane drinking, here's the best preventive Esquire knows: before falling into your spinning bed, dose yourself thoroughly with soda or any of the commercial alkalising salts – and plenty of water.

BLACK VELVET

Half champagne, half stout.

BUILDER-UPPER

In a tall glass filled with ice, insert a long lemon peel – as you would for a Horse's Neck – hooking one end over the edge of the glass. Then put in 2 parts brandy to 1 part Benedictine and fill the glass with ginger ale.

CRIMSON CRINGE

Plain gin with a dash of Grenadine!

FLIPPANT HEN

An egg in a short glass of beer.

PICK-ME-UP

⅓ Dubonnet
⅓ cognac
⅓ Anisette
Lemon peel
White of egg
Cracked ice

Shake well, strain and be picked up.

PRAIRIE OYSTER

1 teaspoon Worcestershire Sauce
Tiny drop Tabasco
1 raw egg
Sprinkling of salt and pepper

Down at a gulp.

Tipples for Teetotalers

SOFT...AND EASY

The secret of entertaining non-drinkers lies in attitude rather than latitude. The only drink-equipment you need is a fruit juice for cocktail-time, a soft drink for hard-drinking-time; but to be a perfect host you need some think-equipment which is sometimes as rare as the guest who doesn't drink.

Think how *you* would feel if, by a great surge of will power, you managed to go on the wagon – then were constantly ridiculed or urged to have 'just one' by well-meaning hosts. Then, when *you're* doing the honours, make it a point never to make a point of abstinence.

Include 'tomato juice' or the like just as you include sherry in that list you rattle off in your 'What'll you have?' speech – so that non-drinkers will know at the outset that their 'foibles' are not going to inconvenience you. Then restrain yourself from comment (including the I-wish-I-had-your-courage sort of false admiration) as you pass the puerile potion. There *are* teetotallers who are also crusaders, but you're not likely to entertain many of them; there are abstainers who smugly revel in praise of their will power, but they're just the ones who'll pour a guilt-edge on other guests if you let them get started.

So, for the good of the party, make no ado about those who do not drink. Have 'dry' drinks available, serve them in glasses like those that pack punch for the other guests, and change the subject.

For the special case, ulcers, for instance, milk is usually in order: and that means just plain milk, without a dash of sympathy. A glass of milk on a tray of Martinis can seldom enter the room without bringing forth the 'little mother' type of so-called humorous remarks – but if you get into the act with a dead-pan, 'Here's your milk punch', at least you leave it up to the ulcerous unfortunate as to whether or not he wants to give his case history. Even if he's hardened to the razzing, he'll appreciate your considerate try to spare him his 10,000th discussion on Ulcers and How I Got One.

Aside from fruit juices, ginger ale, cola and other soda pops, about the only classic teetotaller's tipple you're likely to need is the...

HORSE'S NECK

Peel the whole rind of a lemon, in one spiralling piece. Place it in a tumbler, with one end hanging over the top. Add 2 cubes of ice, a dash of bitters, then fill the tumbler with ginger ale.

MOM COLLINS

When you other guests are drinking Toms, make the same for your dry friend – leaving out only the gin!

...and Be Merry

The Sober Duty of a Host

The mark of a perfect host is that he has a good time at his own party – but not too good. For though he seems to be just another guest, he is really very busy staying sober enough to continue his subtle hosting.

Every man should determine early in life how much liquor he can carry without losing his poise, equilibrium, reputation and civil liberties – but knowledge of his capacity-quotient is particularly important to a host. The amount, of course, is quite variable – depending on the type of liquor, the hour of your last meal, your metabolism and even your mood. Some men can handle with poise and even distinction a half-dozen whisky-and-sodas, while three martinis impel them to pinch the hostess. Others can drink over a half-dozen martinis, but are liable to be left for dead after three whisky-and-sodas. The only way to determine how much you can drink of what, under any given conditions, is by experimentation. But experiment at other people's parties! When you're a host, watch for your own danger-signals with double care.

You've had a few if...

You find yourself thinking up forceful rebuttals for an argument you lost the other day, an argument which, at the time, didn't seem particularly important.

You hold eight diamonds to the ten, jack, a singleton spade and four small clubs and bid one heart, figuring that, although you are vulnerable, a psychic bid, in an effort to save rubber, is a fine strategic move.

There is a fly in your drink, but instead of taking the trouble to remove it, you quaff down your drink, merely taking the precaution to avoid consuming the fly in the process.

The first thing you get when you switch on the radio is a jazz orchestra. You remark that they are playing a swell tune. It turns out to be one which you have heard five or six times previously without being impressed.

You start arguing politics, and make dogmatic statements about economics and sociology although you are by nature a cautious person who customarily qualifies all statements in such a fashion that you always have an out.

You tell that story in mixed company – the one which, when you first heard it, seemed slightly dubious for such an occasion.

It is just before dinner, and your passing dividends have just emptied the shaker. You fail to catch a question from the lady on the sofa next to you because you are wondering if you can get out to the kitchen to mix another batch before dinner.

You hold forth at some length on various celebrities you have encountered lately although you are chronically a person who is impressed by few of them and who actively dislikes the majority.

Dancing with a girl twenty years your junior you try that step which you have seen her Yale escort execute with such precision – and you aren't displeased with the result.

You think it might be fun to send a telegram to somebody.

You sit down at the piano, reel off a couple of tunes, and feel that you are going pretty well. You are delighted when somebody makes a request.

You are in the process of mixing another Tom Collins for yourself. It seems like too much trouble to bother with the lemon squeezer, so you seize half a lemon between your fingers, and squeeze a few drops of juice into your glass. The result tastes all right, although, when starting fresh, you customarily use all the juice you can get out of a whole lemon.

IS THERE A DRUNK IN THE HOUSE?

Since your guests may not be as careful as you to stay on the sober side, you'd best bone up on How to Handle a Drunk on the Premises. Your object, whenever a drunken guest begins to annoy the rest of the party, is to lure the lush into a bedroom and get him to take a nap. 'Let's have a drink in here' or 'I must speak to you alone' are the approaches most likely to succeed. Thereafter, the use of Mickey Finns is not particularly recommended; you can often achieve the same effect with bed or chair combined with just one more very strong slug.

S'PRISE!

Liquor is quicker, but plain old-fashioned hospitality also sets your guests at ease and assures their enjoyment of an evening in your home. Hospitality seems to be composed of two parts sincerity and one part preparedness. In the home of the congenitally good host, no one is ever unexpected. An Emergency Shelf in your pantry should be always equipped to provide a little something for drop-in callers to munch on. The bar is always ready with something to sip. But, most important of all, the host is always ready to pretend he is delighted to have the company of his guests.

Of course, it ain't necessarily so. And sometimes enough is enough.

It may not be Emily Post-ish, but in this busy day it's good sense to know how and when a good host is a poor host. Since the beauty of hospitality is its sincerity, the minute you start wishing people would go home it's time they did. So here are few ways to...

SPEED THE PARTING GUEST

(If you have home movies, you need read no further; just threaten to show them and you'll show even the genus spongae the way to go home.)

1 Turn to your wife or straight-man and say, 'C'mon, c'mon, let's be getting on home so these people can get some sleep.' Then look honestly embarrassed when said wife reminds you, 'Why, we are at home, silly.'

2 When you've planned an evening of quiet or letter-writing and the doorbell rings, put on your hat and coat before you answer the door. 'Why hello, hello! Gee, I wish you had let me know you were coming over; I'm already late for such and such. I was just leaving; can't I drop you somewhere?'

3 After an uninvited house guest has taken complete charge of your household, rearranged your furniture, run up a cross-country phone bill, charged all his laundry and cleaning to you, killed your dog with cakes and candy....there's only one way to get rid of him.

   Tell him you are moving, have all the furniture loaded on a big red van and tell the driver to keep driving the furniture around the block until your guest has left. This may cost you a fortune, but it will save you a nervous breakdown.

4 When your cocktail guests have stayed long past the dinner hour, when you're sick of cigarette smoke and gags that don't sound so side-splitting any more, make sure that there's an adequate liquid supply on hand, announce that you're late for your dinner date, and just go out into the night. Not very cordial, but often the only tactics to adopt unless you're willing to have your cocktail party turned into a supper party – and perhaps even a breakfast.

5 Even before the over-staying guest finishes his statement, agree – instantly, uncharacteristically and with only a slightly impatient tone in your 'yes, yes'.

6 Fix the radio: 'You don't mind? I've been meaning to do this for weeks.' Or, better still, fix the clock and keep asking what time it is. Even if the ruse fails, the evening will not have been wasted – provided, of course, that clock or radio needs fixing.

7 Arrange with your dog to demand to be taken out, so you can explain, smiling weakly, 'We always walk the dog just before bedtime; guess he thinks I've forgotten him.' With appropriate 'There-there Duke – we'll go out soon's' in the dog's direction, of course.

BE PREPARED

When your guests are expected, and of course welcome, you'll enjoy the gathering more yourself if you make sure that everything is in readiness before your guests arrive. Cooking underway, table set, ice and liquor ready, ash trays out, canapés ready to serve, etc. It's usually safest to dress first, finish your last-minute chores later, in case anyone arrives early; then you'll at least appear to be ready.

Once the party has officially begun, your major job is to keep it from breaking up into cliques or settling down into polite boredom. For a good start, provide your guests with a conversational opening the very moment you introduce them; don't settle for 'Miss Jones, this is Mr. Collins,' but add something like 'Tom has just come back from Washington, Jane. He can probably bring you up to date on your old hangouts.' From there, of course, Mr Collins has to find out why Miss Jones should be so familiar with Washington night-life, and Miss Jones must ask about his trip. Before they finish playing 'do-you-know?' they'll be old friends.

If one of your guests is shy or a stranger or both, draft him or her as your assistant. When she has something to pass or to do, the shy girl will be forced out of her corner and made to feel a part of the group in spite of herself. The same technique sometimes works in breaking up cliques: you can call one or two people away from a closed group, put them to doing some small thing like picking out the next records to be played, and then introduce new people to the old group.

Incidentally, as host you yourself should avoid being caught in a long discussion or an entrenched circle. But unlike the guests, whom you must sometimes rescue from monologists or drunks, you can always break away if necessary with a simple 'Excuse me. Be back as soon as I can.' Be as much of a free agent as you can, rushing in where a host's soothing words or a change of subject seems indicated.

And then there's the classic trick for causing guests to circulate: put the food at one end of the room and the drink at the other.

GOOD TALK

Whatever the sort of gathering in your home, the major entertainment will very likely be conversation. As a mere human being, of course, you should know the ins and outs of good conversation. As a host, such knowledge is essential, for one of your jobs is to steer the talk. You will, of course, make sure that the conversation at no time excludes any one of your guests – the comparative stranger who doesn't know the people under discussion, say, or the athlete who is quite naturally fidgeting after prolonged conversation about art. You will create openings for the shy, switch subjects where neces-

sary to bring the talk into line with one quiet guest's background, squelch shoptalk when it ceases to furnish interesting titbits for the uninitiated and becomes instead a lecture or a technical discussion. You won't let the conversation embarrass any guest; you'll soothe tempers and act as arbiter if arguments get out of hand.

For this job of steering conversation, perhaps the prime qualification is to be a good conversationalist yourself. And who is a good conversationalist?

His talk is casual, easy, varied. He rarely talks for more than three minutes at a time unless others ask questions to keep him going.

He suits his topics to his audiences. He does not drag out his personal affairs or his innermost convictions for casual acquaintances. With them he can keep up a perfect, enjoyable chatter about the weather, the caprices of Rhode Island Reds or yesterday's front-page murder. He'll talk about bridge only to those who play bridge, about a new play only to those who have seen the play. He reserves intimate conversation for intimate friends. When he tells you something, you have a feeling he thought it would interest *you*, not that he wanted to tell it to *somebody*.

His phrases are crisp, his remarks have a beginning and an end. And no rambling by-paths.

It's not easy to put a finger on his success. But this you know: when you have said good-bye you realise you have had a good time. You never emerge from his house with a worse opinion of yourself than when you entered. You could almost believe that he hadn't noticed the idiotic remarks you made during the talk on Italian submarines.

In retrospect you remember two things:

That he listened with brilliant intensity. It was flattering to talk in the face of such attention.

Those few wisecracks or jokes cling to your memory. You laughed when he said to the too-fertile lady novelist: 'Good God, my dear woman, are you with book again?' And his answer when someone slyly accused him of being involved in a scandal: 'It's very flattering but untrue. We're strictly perpendicular friends.' You smiled frequently but the remarks always fitted specific cases. There was little that could be lifted from its context and repeated in another conversation.

Working toward that general goal, it would be well to remember these Eight Cardinal Sins of Conversation:

1. 'He was an old varlet.'

Anyone who tosses rare, obsolete words into his conversation makes his listeners pay less attention to what he says than how he says it. But pedantry isn't the only form of conversational snobbery. Sometimes a man who did brilliantly in Professor Snitchkins' English IV chooses to say, 'I ain't', 'I knowed him', 'I went for to see him', because these expressions sounded amusing when spoken by a rustic. Some forms of speech like some vintages of wine don't travel well.

2. 'So I had a Winer Kaffee.'

How many English-speaking people know what this means? How many know *corrida, Weltanschauung, oi sunetoi, dolce far niente, béguin, en papillotes, quid pro quo, Wanderjahr, flaneur*?

Foreign words unless anglicised or clearly known to the majority of educated people should be shunned. Unless the speaker wants to be considered a snob.

3. 'So he said, "Come along."'

'And I said, "I simply can't."'
'And he said, "Why not?"'
'"Why?" I said. "Because I made a date with Eddie."'

Edith Wharton made the observation that good novelists use dialogue sparingly – only when it is desirable to tell the exact words spoken by a character. The same holds for conversation. Yards of dialogue can sometimes be summed up in a foot of narrative. The above phrases could better be said, 'He urged me to come but I explained I had an engagement'. Half the words and clearer expression.

4. 'I got into New York at seven and then this man took me to dinner at the Waldorf.'

Well, *what* man? It is sometimes perfect technique to keep the characters in one's conversation anonymous but references to 'these people', 'this friend', 'somebody I know' give the conversation a curious blurred quality and make the speaker sound like a sneak.

There are two ways to introduce characters into conversation. One is to be crisply anonymous: 'A friend of mind told me that...' (not 'this friend'), 'a cousin of mine wanted to play tennis', 'a red-headed harridan who sat next to me on the bus'.

But occasionally a story should be better documented. The method, then, is to start off at the beginning:

'I had written a letter to a man named George Redwood in Cleveland. The day I got there I sent the letter and the next morning he phoned, asking me to lunch with him. He's about thirty-five, unmarried. He's a lawyer, writes articles for law journals. He's a golf champ, too, so when he suggested we play at his club...'

Or:

'You've heard me speak to Ted Gorham, my roommate in college. He's just busted into the movies so when I was in Hollywood I phoned him. He was having a party and invited me over. That's how I met...'

It ought to be easy to decide when to introduce characters by name with a brief account of their works and achievements. In general, characters who enter a conversation briefly and casually should be left nameless. If the speaker intends to refer to them constantly they should be identified at the outset.

5. 'That reminds me.'

People are reminded of altogether too many things in conversation. If the talk is about the Spanish Revolution and someone is reminded that Aunt Esther's janitor is a Spaniard, the conversation is done for. Every time 'that reminds me' flashes through the cerebrum, it should be followed by an examination of conscience: 'I'm reminded of something, yes, but has it anything to do with the subject in hand?' If the answer is no, self-control is required. If that looks dubious, the reminded one should stop up to the cocktail bar and silently repeat 'that reminds me' with each sip until the attack has passed off.

6. 'William Powell was in it. It started off in Singapore where he was a beachcomber. Then there was an explosion...'

There must be a special compartment in hell for people who related the plots of movies, books and plays. And in this compartment there must be a special chamber with a thermostat apparatus keeping the temperature at 3,000 Fahrenheit for those who are too sophisticated to reel off plots from beginning to end but who don't hesitate to prattle about special scenes: 'There's something remarkable about the novel – *in spots*. For instance the scene when the uncle confronts his nephew with the evidences of the theft. A terrific mistral was blowing. It was set in Nice, you see.'

7. 'Do you get the point?'

There's only one proper reply to people who say, 'Do you get the point?' 'Do you follow?' 'Sure you understand what I mean?' It is 'I doubt if there is any point but in any case I'm not following and of course I don't understand what you mean.'

8. 'I'm not boring you, am I?'

What does the speaker expect? What would he do if he got a truthful answer? The very suspicion that one is boring another ought to freeze up the tongue.

But sometimes a speaker will say, 'I'm not boring you, am I?' when he knows very well he's interesting everyone in sight. The motive is sometimes nervousness, sometimes a mistaken idea of making a dramatic pause. It provides a second good reason for not asking people if you are boring them. In every company there are some individuals who don't know whether they are bored or spellbound. Suggest boredom and they'll yawn. They are the kind who would be bored by the spectacle of George Bernard Shaw eating a cannibal.

These general precepts hold good whatever the subject of conversation – but when you get into serious discussion you need additional rules. If you and your friends are content with cocktail-party chit-chat and aimless talk about personalities and personal experiences, skip this next section. But if you would like either to improve your own batting average in serious discussion or to use your home as a gathering place for friends who like large talk, the following suggestions of Mortimer Adler may prove invaluable.

HOW TO TALK SENSE IN COMPANY

From an Esquire article by Mortimer J. Adler, professor at the University of Chicago and author of *How to Read a Book*.

A distinguished educator recently pointed out a paradox about our country. We have achieved wonders in mechanical communication, but human communication has been breaking down. People still gather socially, but more and more they turn to the radio or bridge; and if they talk, they tend either to talk about trivial things or, if they begin talking about serious matters, they tend to get into bitter and fruitless disputes. Yet there are rules for good conversation – rules which make discussion both pleasurable and profitable. To be able to persuade someone to see a point your way – to win his agreement by moving his mind, not by bludgeoning or intimidating him – is certainly as pleasant as winning at bridge or golf through an exercise of skill. To learn something as a result of being genuinely open to persuasion is profitable use of conversational time.

Now the rules, even though they are 'ideals', are neither hard to understand nor impossible to follow. The next time you meet with your friends and begin discussing, say, politics, why not place a copy of these rules in the hands of the coolest-headed member of the group? Appoint him chief umpire and bouncer. See if it doesn't make a difference.

I. Beginning a Discussion

Pick the right occasion. There are times for small talk and times, so to speak, for big talk. A dinner party is a bad place for big talk. Whenever conversation must be larded in between other activities, such as going to the theatre and going to bed, it might just as well be trivial. You must always have plenty of time. Good talk is usually slow in getting started and long in winding up. A gathering in which many of those present are strangers is usually a small-talk group. An evening of relaxation, when most of those present are tired, is no occasion to solve the problems of the world. But when friends are gathered and they share an impulse to talk about their common problems, then serious discussion can take place.

Pick the right people. Don't try to discuss everything with everybody. Even some of your best friends may lack competence on certain subjects. Some people aren't interested in some subjects. Some people 'just don't get along together'. If you happen know that Green and Robinson hate each other, keep the conversation on the weather.

Don't argue to win. Of course, you want to persuade, but you should also be open to persuasion. Good discussion is an exchange, not a blitzkrieg.

Don't argue for argument's sake. Don't pick an argument on every point regardless of what you really think. Don't disagree just to keep the argument going. Better taper off into small talk before everyone is antagonised and discussion becomes a feud.

Don't be polite. Discussions are often nipped in the bud because people don't want to quarrel. They suppose you can't argue without losing your temper. They don't want to quarrel with their friends, but the minor agony of examining a difference of opinion is one of the best expressions of friendship. Those who are willing to take pains in honest and forthright discussion are helping, not offending, each other.

Don't listen only to yourself. Don't sit around thinking of a bright remark with which to break in and win applause. It is not your private train of thought which matters most. Of course, you may get a good idea at a moment when someone else is making a long speech. It is hard to be patient – but it is the only way to talk sense.

II. Carrying on a Discussion

Find out what the issue is. Until the issue is clear, it is impossible to tell what points are relevant and what are not. The best way to make the issue explicit is to state it.

Take one thing at a time. This is a good rule in talking, as it is in living. Every serious problem has many angles. Our first obligation is to separate a jumble of related questions into a number of distinct issues. Let's say you are discussing religion. Cover, say, the historical question about church origins before you take up the theological question about church doctrine, and that before you consider the political question about church practices.

Stick to the issue. Irrelevance is the rock on which most conversations are wrecked. The worst of it is that, unless everyone is on the lookout for it, the victims don't realise before it's too late that they got off the course.

Keep moving. After a point has been settled push on to the next one. This doesn't mean you shouldn't come back to a point if it needs reopening. But it does mean a conversation should be a progress. The man who hasn't listened attentively usually raises from the dead some point that was settled. Backing and filling is one of the mortal diseases of conversation.

Don't take things for granted. Since few conversations begin at the beginning, and something is usually taken for granted, the rules might be better stated as follows: ask your companions to grant the assumptions you are making. We frequently suspect that the other fellow is making assumptions, though precisely what they are we seldom know. We too infrequently recognise that we ourselves are also making assumptions. If you see the point of this rule, you also see that all argument is either about the assumptions themselves or their consequences. I can grant your premises, and still think you have reached a wrong conclusion.

Don't disagree until you understand. Unless you can state the other fellow's position just as well as he can, you have no right to oppose him. The man who says, 'Now look here, you're saying...' usually mis-states the other fellow's position. Begin, 'Let me see if I can state your position', and unless he agrees that you've done it, you can't tell him he's wrong.

Don't agree until you understand. To agree with something you don't understand is inane. We all have the tendency, at times, to say 'Uh huh', when we should be saying 'Wait a minute – I'm not sure I get you straight'. Most of us are too prone to suppose we understand. Moving on to the next point is important, but we should not agree just for the sake of moving on.

Don't take a vote. A majority of your friends may, at any given moment, be wrong. Everyone in the party may disagree with you, and you may still be right. And you can be wrong even if the majority agree with you. Counting noses settles nothing except the numbers of Ayes and Nays. Voting may follow arguing, but it should never take the place of argument.

Beware of examples. 'Why, I know a fellow who...' Everyone knows a fellow who. Examples may be helpful, but they may just as often be harmful. And the discussion starts going in circles when, after you've cited an example, everybody else cites one to prove something else. An example is like an assumption. You ought to ask permission to use it. Unless everyone sees its direct relevance, it can do no good.

Never argue about facts. If you have doubts about a fact someone has cited, express them, but don't argue. If you have time, look up the exact size of the national debt, or the flight time to Paris. If that cannot be done, accept the dubious fact for the purpose of discussion.

Explain your disagreement. If, after you understand the other fellow's position, you still disagree, you do so for one or more of the following reasons: You think that he simply lacks knowledge of some relevant point; or that he mistakenly supposes he has knowledge when he doesn't; or that he drew the wrong conclusions from things you were willing to admit were so; or that he drew the right conclusions but didn't push them far enough. Disagreement never gives way to agreement unless the difference is located. Trying to define it helps you find out when the disagreement is only apparent, due to your divergent use of words.

III. Ending the Discussion

Don't expect too much from discussion. If you engage in argument with no hope of reaching agreement, you expect too little. If you suppose agreement can always be reached, you expect too much. Reasonable men can agree wherever knowledge is possible, but there are many matters about which even reasonable men can only entertain opinions.

Distinguish between theoretical and practical questions. This helps you follow the preceding rule. Whether 2 plus 2 equals 4 is what is known as a theoretical question. When you discuss problems of this sort, you should expect agreement on the truth. But when you discuss practical problems, problems which concern what should be done in this case, you are in the realm of opinion. Here honest, intelligent men, trying to be reasonable, may disagree.

Distinguish between principles and cases. The general principles we must appeal to in arguing questions of policy are always true everywhere and for all men. Reasonable men can agree about the nature of justice; but they can disagree indefinitely about whether a certain business deal was just or unjust.

Don't stop with agreement. Argument is not only form of profitable conversation. Men who agree can often help each other clarify a point by discussing it. Conversation is a useful device for exploring a theme about which there is general agreement. You may all agree that Fascism is a bad form of government yet spend many evenings helping each other discover the reasons why. People who stop talking when they agree seldom probe their beliefs very deeply.

Don't go on forever. Even in matters where agreement is possible, discussion sometimes reaches an impasse. When you see it is fruitless to go on, change the subject. If the conversation is paralysed by the obstinacy of the opponents, let it die naturally.

These three sets of rules are what might be called the technical precepts for talking sense. They direct you in the use of your mind. But these technical rules will be useless unless you can also follow the 'emotional rules'.

Of course, our emotions play an important role in everything we do and say. But they don't help us talk sense. When you find yourself getting excited or angry during a conversation, take a trip to the water cooler. If that does not help, stand up and say, 'Friends, I'm sore as a boil. I'm hitting below the belt, but I can't help it. I'm mad.' It will do you good, and the rest will admire you for admitting it.

If another member of the group gets fighting mad, you have only two alternatives. Soothe him in a friendly way. If that does not work, change the subject. He's probably just as nice a fellow as you are, but someone happened to hit him in a tender spot. Get off the spot. The barkeeper's advice, 'If you want to fight, you've got to fight outside', is indispensable to good conversation.

And how to do you know when your emotions are getting the better of you?

First, you find yourself shouting the other fellow down. Or you stop thinking and merely repeat your claim over and over, each time with greater heat and less light.

Second, you find yourself making irrelevant references to his grandmother, his nationality, his occupation or his personal habits. This is to argue against the man, rather than against his ideas. The most exasperating form is the bedfellow argument. You say, 'So you agree with Hitler', as if that necessarily made the other fellow wrong.

Third, you find yourself being sarcastic, or trying to get the laugh on your opponent, or baiting him by harping on unimportant mistakes he has made. All these devices are calculated to goad your opponent into losing his temper also. If he resists all your efforts, and keeps cool, he will probably enrage you further.

Fourth, you will find yourself suppressing points which you see, but will weaken your case.

Finally, you find yourself stubbornly refusing to admit what you see, namely, that you are in the wrong. By this time you cannot remember the wise counsel that there is no point in winning an argument, or even in standing pat, when you know you're wrong. Unfortunately, you will remember it after the evening is over, when passions have cooled. If you let yourself get out of hand this way very often, you will eventually ruin your disposition.

By following these rules, and controlling your emotions in order to do so, you will find pleasure and profit in serious conversation. the better you follow them, the more pleasure and profit.

HOW ATTRACTIVE
ARE YOU TO WOMEN?

1   Do you show your real fondness for a girl by telling her about her bad points and advising her how to improve them?
This is an error. If you must tell her you hate her perfume or how she does her hair, wrap it up in heavy sugar coating.

2   Do you have a double code about drunkenness for men and women when they are together?
If a man has to get drunk, he'll be more attractive if he restricts this behaviour to stag company.

3   Do you make distinctions between the jokes you'd tell a man in the club shower and those you'd tell a girl in a parked automobile?
Almost no women like bathroom jokes or jokes with dirty words.

4   Do you tell a woman she's beautiful, even if she isn't?
This habit hurts nobody and makes a lot of girls happier.

5   Do you plan your evenings with a woman ahead of time or leave the choice of amusement up to her?
It's much more flattering for a man to announce the evening's programme, showing he has given thought to her amusement.

6   Do you believe it necessary in the modern age to push in a girl's chair for her and to light her cigarettes?
These small courtesies mean a lot to a girl.

7   Do you ever tell a girl you love her, under the spell of the moment, when you suspect that you won't tomorrow?
This is a dirty trick and if you do, you ought to be ashamed of yourself. Moreover, the word will soon get around to other women.

8 How many times a week do you shave?
Once a day is a minimum, if you care what women think of you.

9   Would you dine a girl expensively and not buy her flowers, or economise on the place and bring her at least a gardenia?
Most women would prefer having flowers and less to eat.

10 Do you try to arouse a girl's interest by boasting of your success with other women?
Don't ever do this!

11 Do you use the continental approach, based on the belief that an immediate pass flatters a woman?
This is the average man's greatest mistake. If a pass on first acquaintance doesn't insult a girl it at least bores her.

12 Can you describe the dress worn by the last two girls you took out?
If not, notice and comment on the next few. Women appreciate having men notice the efforts they make over their appearance.

13 Do you sometimes take a girl out in parties of four or more, as a change from a twosome?
A good idea. A girl may feel hurt if you never ask her to meet your other friends.

14 Do you ask an attractive girl, who is probably busy most evenings, to call you up sometime when she's free?
Don't do this: you should always ask a popular girl far enough ahead of time to find a free evening.

15 If your hostess at a dance is obviously having a whirl, do you consider it necessary to dance with her?
You always should, as a matter of good manners.

16 Do you consider it a young girl's own business whether she gets tight and is indiscreet when she's out with you?
Keep an inexperienced girl from getting tight, and don't let any woman become indiscreet through liquor. Triumphs over drunken women don't help any man.

17 If a girl you're fond of asks you to be nice to her cousin with adenoids and buck teeth do you cut her off your list?
Not pleasant, but if you rally round and give Cousin Belle a whirl, you'll soon be known as the nicest man in town.

18 If you had a quarrel with a girl will you wait for her to apologize before calling her up or risk being a door mat and do it first?
Be a door mat – it's easier for you to call a girl than for her to call you.

HOW ATTRACTIVE
ARE YOU TO MEN?

1   Do you bring the names of other men into the conversation to give yourself a sought-after appearance?
Don't. This may give a man a sense of inferiority – he is uncomfortable with you, and soon drifts away to someone else. It may make him wonder how much talking you do about him.

2   Do you wear clothes that make you a little more up-to-the-minute than the other women in your set?
Good – provided your taste is reliable and that the clothes suit you. Men may rant about that 'crazy hat' but they swell with pride when their lady companions arouse admiring stares.

3   If you are asked to get another girl for a foursome, do you pick one obviously less attractive than you are?
You are unwise to do so. Get the most glamorous girl you know, and both men will be pleased.

4   Do you make a point of building up other women, even those you dislike in discussing them with a man?
This is sound practice. But don't put it on so thick that it sounds like a line.

5   Do men marvel at your capacity for holding liquor?
A great mistake: it gives you a fast reputation and runs into money – the man's money – besides.

6   Do you keep men interested by hinting that later – not tonight – you'll be really demonstrative?
This is a low trick and one that a surprising number of men see through at once. If you kiss a man it should be for your own pleasure and not a reward for him.

7   Do you make things easier for a man by suggesting that he climb into a car first, if he's driving, or by asking him not to stand up when you come into the room?
This is an error – men know that they are supposed to show these signs of consideration to a girl and the respect her more if she takes them as a matter of course.

8 Do you ever embarrass a man by telling him he's good-looking or has big muscles or is too, too intelligent?
Try it! Almost any man can stand almost any amount of flattery, however obvious, without embarrassment or suspicion.

9 Do you knit when you are having a cozy, fireside evening with a man?
For some reason, men hate to see a woman doing anything with her hands when talking to her. Undivided attention is best.

10 Do you either play bridge or dance really well?
If not, take steps to correct this at once. You're better off if you do both well, but one talent is mandatory.

11 Are you so beautifully groomed that you make the average man feel like a lout when he takes you out?
Fine. Men are extremely critical of any imperfection in a girl's neatness. If he feels like a lout once, the average escort will take pains to be better dressed himself the next time.

12 Do you keep your friendships warm by chatty calls to your men friends at their offices?
This is fatal.

13 Do you use artificial conversation gambits like 'What movie would you choose if you had to see it every week for a year?' to start talk with a shy dinner partner?
A very good plan – someone has to start the conversation and a question like this can keep it rolling for quite a while.

14 Do you save yourself wear and tear by not troubling to entertain men bores?
A grave mistake. Bores have their uses since a clever girl can practice her conversation on them, with nothing much to lose. Besides, they often have attractive friends.

15 How many comfortable chairs are there in your living room?
At least two, I hope. No man can fall in love unless he has a chance to relax and he can't if either of you sits bolt upright.

16 Do you suffer from indecision when ordering dinner or drinks in a restaurant with a man?
This maddens them: learn to make up your mind rapidly.

Games

THE LIFE-SAVERS OF THE PARTY

There comes a time in every host's life when conversation is better replaced by GAMES. When your guests know each other so well that they have nothing new to say to each other...when your guests are such complete strangers that they seem in dire need of an organised ice breaker...when your guests, friends or strangers, are of such divergent views and interest that a normal conversation may result in hopeless agreement or boredom, propose a game.

The easiest games of all to organise are that involve the minimum of props and which can be relied upon to end after a finite period of time. There is no point in suggesting a fascinating board game if the board in question is at someone else's apartment. And nobody will be particularly keen to embark on a marathon epic of a game which looks likely to last into the wee small hours of the morning. Much better to organise a game that will pass half an hour or so. If your guests have enjoyed it you can suggest a repeat, if not you can move on to another game entirely.

All in all, the most suitable and versatile prop for games is a pack of cards. The rudiments of most games can be picked up relatively quickly and, in any case, most of your guests will already know how to play the standard games. Try to keep in your desk at least two packs of relatively new, unthumbed cards. You will probably only need one at a time, but accidents can happen to cards – especially after a few drinks. And, no matter how tempting it might seem, never proffer your friends a pack of marked cards. If you are rumbled, they will stop being your friends forthwith.

Here are few suggestions, most of which can be adapted to the evening-for-two (either as a prop for the benefit of unexpected callers or as a genuine device for passing the early evening) as well as to the gang gathering.

CARD GAMES

BELOTE: THE OLD FRENCH GAME

Here's the Gin Rummy sequel for which it was necessary to go back to the days of Madame Pompadour. It moves faster than bridge and has an essence of poker. Here is a complete set of rules for Belote as presented in an Esquire article by P. C. Elston:

Belote is played with thirty-two cards and a box of chips. You diminish the fifty-two card deck for Belote by throwing out the twos, threes, fours, fives, and sixes. Belote can be played by two, three, four or five persons, and there is no dummy except when five play. The object is to make your contract, or to prevent your opponents from making theirs. If, after naming the trump, that side fails to fulfil its contract (to make more points than the other side), then all of the points of the one who has named the trump are scored by the other side.

POINTS

1. All tens rank above all kings, coming just below aces. 2. In the trump suit, and in the trump suit only, jack is the high card and nine is the next. The others follow in regular order: ace, ten, king, etc. Points are scored as follows: each ace, 11; each ten, 10; each king, 4; each queen, 3; each of three jacks, 2; jack of trumps, 20; nine of trumps, 14; bonus for taking last trick, 10. Total 162.

In addition to the 162 regular points there are 'announcement' points which add excitement to the game in giving luck a priority over skill. These announcement points are:

Belotete – king and queen of trumps held in same hand	20
Tierce – any straight flush of three held in same hand	20
Cinquante – any straight flush of four held in same hand	50
Cent – any straight flush of five held in same hand	100
Four aces, tens, kings or queens held in same hand	100
Four nines, held in same hand	150
Four jacks, held in same hand	200

Fours of a kind outrank straight flushes.

DEAL AND BID: The dealer gives two cards together to each player, and then three. He turns the twenty-first card up and bidding then starts. By bidding we mean simply the accepting of the card turned up as the trump, or passing. All suits have the same value. The bidding is started, not by the dealer, but by the player on his right. The successful bidder takes the exposed card into his hand. That gives him six cards and he has two more to be dealt to him before the bidding is over. Each of the other players has three more to be dealt to him. This bidding on a partial hand, with two cards yet to come, gives a poker flavour to the game.

THE BIDDING: Since the regular points are 162, and you have a partner to help you, it is reasonable to name a trump if you see as many as forty probable points in the first six cards. In making this estimate, possession of three out of eight trumps may be given a value of ten, in addition to the points that may be scored by the individual cards. With less than forty in sight, it is more prudent to pass.

The first round of bidding is on the suit of the exposed card only. If all four players decline to accept that suit as trump, each one passes; then, on the second round, any other suit may be named. If all pass for the second time, then it is a new deal. If a bid has been made, then the remaining cards are dealt out, two only to the bidder (who has picked up the exposed card), and three to the other players.

PLAY: No matter who has made the trump, play is started by the player on the right of the dealer. It is while the first trick is being played that announcements are made. Any player who has one to make should make it as he plays his first card on the first trick. After his first card has fallen on the table it is too late. This is a feature that calls for strict attention. The only exception to this rule is in the case of the 'belote' announcement; that is, king and queen of trumps held in the same hand. The announcement should be made by saying 'belote', and later 'rebelote', as the trump king and queen are played out. The reason for this will appear later.

ANNOUNCEMENTS: Announcements are valid in accordance with their rank. Thus, if the player who plays first announces a tierce, and the opponents make a higher announcement, then the first announcement does not count. In the case of two or more tierces it is the highest one that counts, the ranking of the cards in this matter being precisely as in poker, the ten taking its normal position between jack and nine. If announcements are of equal rank, the one announced first prevails unless the one announced later is in the trump suit. Partners' announcements score concurrently; that is, if you hold the highest one you thereby validate any lower one that may be held by your partner, even if his is lower than one held by your opponents. There may be, of course, two tierces in the same hand. Both count in case the higher one is the highest one announced. Immediately after the first trick is played, all valid announcements must be laid face up on the table. When all have seen them, they are taken back into the player's hand and play proceeds. The exposed trump card should also be left on the table until after the first trick is completed.

Announcements, since they add to the total score, increase the liability of the biding side. Thus an announcement of 100 lifts the total score to 262 and makes it necessary for the bidders to make 132 points in order to fulfil their contract.

No-trump: This is a spicy feature. It cannot be an original bid. It can be bid only after another suit has been named for trump. When any player names a suit for trump, he thereby opens the door for a no-trump bid, which is the only overbid. If the exposed card is an ace, it is obviously dangerous to name that suit for trumps unless you are protected by another ace already in your hand, for the probability is that your opponents will pick up the free ace on the board and declare no-trump. The possession of two aces is a minimum warrant for a no-trump bid.

After a suit has been named for trumps, the other players in proper turn should say 'pass' or 'no-trump' before play starts. If any player says 'no trump' out of turn, that should annul the hand because too much information has been given thereby.

You can go no-trump over your partner's bid as well as over your opponents'. It is conventional to do so if you have a minimum of two aces, or one ace with an announcement of fifty or better. Usually a better score will be made this way than if you leave your partner in with his original bid.

The attraction and the risk in a no-trump bid lie in the fact that its *score is doubled*. Since the trump value of jack and nine are out, all four aces being high cards with tens next, the total score without announcements is 130 instead of 162, but the doubling brings this up to 260. The score of all announcements is also doubled. Last trick, being doubled, counts 20, and is usually more important in no-trump hands than in trump hands. In fact the winning or losing of a no-trump bid is very likely to depend upon which side takes the last trick, and careful attention needs to be given to the cards that are out.

One convention in connection with no-trump bidding is worth bearing in mind. It occurs when the exposed card is an ace and, on the first round, all players have declined to name that suit trumps. If, on the second round of bidding, your partner names some other suit trump, that is a command for you to take up the ace on the table and declare no-trump. The presumption is that your partner has at least one strong suit to the ace. Of course, the player between your partner and yourself may go no-trump, and thus relieve you of further responsibility as to the bidding.

BYLAWS: It is obligatory, in case you cannot follow suit, to trump, unless you have no trumps or your partner is master of the trick. Of course, you must play a trump card if trumps have been led; and, even though your partner may be master of the trick, you *must trump over him* if you hold a *higher trump* than the one he has played. It is obligatory to over-trump if possible whenever trumps have been led, or whenever an opponent has become master of a trick in which you cannot follow in the suit that has been led. If you cannot follow in a suit that has been led, and an opponent has trumped it, *you also must trump* even though compelled to play a trump lower than his.

A tie score is called at *litige*. In this case, the non-bidders score their points, but the points of the bidders are held in suspense until the next hand has been played, and then awarded to the winners of that hand.

When one side takes all the tricks it is called *capote*. In that case a bonus of one hundred points is awarded to the winning side, but the ten bonus for the last trick is not counted. A capote in no-trump scores two hundred points. This capote feature affects the play of the hand. When you see that there is a chance to make a capote, you should play to make it, rather than prudently salvaging cards that risk being trumped. Usually one saves tens, but sometimes one misses a capote by doing so.

In case of capote, the side that has no tricks has no claim on the score of the other side even though by virtue of *announcements* it may have a larger score. Nor can a side that has taken no tricks win a game on that hand even though its announcement points carry its total core beyond the goal that has been agreed upon; in such a case, all points count, but an additional hand must be played to determine the winner. In other words, you cannot go out when you are capoted.

BELOTE AND REBELOTE: As stated before, the announcement of 'belote' is made as the king and queen that compose it are played, belote being called for the first one played, and rebelote for the second. Since belote is not scored unless it is properly announced, if the bidding side sees that it is going to be set, and if one of that side holds the belote, that player may prefer not to say 'rebelote', thus avoiding the risk of giving twenty additional points to the opponents. On the other hand, announcement of 'rebelote' may just save being set. In such an event one needs to know how the points are running. In case of a decision not to announce 'rebelote' it is better, in order to avoid possible misunderstanding, to make the statement: 'I am not announcing rebelote' as the second card (king or queen) is played.

The 'arrête' is a feature that often has dramatic value at the end of a close game. Suppose the play is for 1,200 points. One side has 1,160, and the other 1,170. Play starts. As soon as either side has taken in enough game points (not announcement points) to make a total of 1,200, a player of that side may say 'j'arrête'. That ends the game, even in the middle of the play of a hand, unless the side that says 'j'arrête' is the side that has bid, in which case the hand must be played out to make sure whether the contract is fulfilled or not. This 'arrête' feature may enable the side that has the weaker cards on the last hand to nose out a victory by reaching the goal before their opponents pass it. On such a hand it is, of course, a great advantage to have the first play and to make all possible scores as quickly as can be done.

WHEN PLAYED BY THREE

In the three-handed game each player is for himself. the contract is to make more points than either, but not both, of the other players. In case of failure to do so, the contractor's points go to that player who has the highest score. In case of capote, the player who takes no tricks scores no game points and each of the players scores an additional fifty points; but the player who is capoted is entitled to his announcement points unless he is the one who has made the contract. In the event that two players are capote, the player who has taken all the tricks scores one hundred extra points.

Six cards are dealt, three at a time, to each player before the biding starts, and three afterwards. Thus the play is with nine cards in each hand instead of eight.

The exposed card does not go automatically into the hand of the bidder, as in the four-handed game, but even in case the suit of that card has been names as trump, the exposed card can be 'bought' by any player who has the seven of that suit, the seven being laid down when the exposed card is taken up. This may be done either before or after the last cards are dealt, but it must be done before play starts. After the last cards are dealt, the bottom card is also exposed. This is merely to reduce the number of unknown and undealt cards to three.

After each hand has been played, each player's score must be counted separately on account of the cards that are not in play.

WHEN PLAYED BY TWO

The two-handed game observes the same rules as the three-handed game except that there are twelve unknown and undealt cards. In case of capote, one hundred additional points are taken by the winner. To deal is a slight disadvantage since the non-dealer has first bid. For that reason it is a rule that the deal goes to or remains with the winner of the preceding hand. In case of no bidding, the deal changes hands.

Since there are twelve undealt cards, the two-handed game invites the taking of greater risks than the three- or four-handed game.

WHEN PLAYED BY FIVE

This is a highly sociable form of Belote. The dealer sits out. This involves a shift in partnerships on each hand, and individual scores are kept. More chips are needed. A game is not completed, no matter what the score, until each player has been the dealer as often as any other player.

GIN RUMMY

Here's Gin Rummy, the card craze that crashed the gates of Hollywood, and travelled east like a prairie fire. Perhaps you 'thumbs down' these Esquire rules, but after consulting a crop of crack players, we decided there must be a different variation for every player. So instead of using Betty Grable's method, here is a set of rules compiled by Esquire, which we hope will end all conflicts and shilly-shally at the Gin Rummy table:

RULES FOR PLAYING GIN RUMMY FOR
TWO, THREE OR FOUR PLAYERS

THE PACK is a full pack of fifty-two cards, which rank in sequence from king (high) down to the ace. In scoring, kings, queens, jacks and tens count 10 points each, all other cards their face value; aces are 1. Suits have no rank.

NUMBER OF PLAYERS – two, except as described below under 'Gin Rummy for Three Players' and 'Gin Rummy for Four Players'.

Deal – Ten cards, one at a time. After a deal, the next card is turned face up on the table to begin the discard pile (the talon) and the remainder of the deck is placed beside it, face down, to form the stock.

OBJECT OF THE GAME – To form sequences of three or more cards in the same suit (as four, five and six of hearts) and combinations of three or four cards of a kind (as three or four kings).

PLAY – Beginning with dealer's opponent (pone), each player in turn draws one card from the talon or stock; after the draw, he discards a card from his hand face up on the talon to maintain his hand at ten cards. At the beginning of the deal, if pone refuses the turned-up card, dealer may take it; if both refuse, pone draws from the stock.

Play continues in this way, with each player attempting to improve his hand, until the end of the deal; in the meantime, neither player may meld (place on the table) any sequences or combinations, but must keep them in his hand. The deal ends when one of the players scores a down as described below, or until all except two cards in the stock have been exhausted (in the latter case, game is a draw and no one scores).

THE DOWN – When a player can meld enough cards so that his remaining, unmatched cards add up to 10 or less (as four, three and ace), he may declare a down by exposing his cards and announcing the points he has remaining, doing this after making his draw and at the same time he makes his discard. Opponent then melds all his sequences and combinations and in addition may also 'lay off' by playing cards on the other player's melds. Opponent then announces his remaining points; score for the deal is the difference between these points and those of the player who declared the down.

SCORING – Player who declares the down wins the hand and receives credit for the score, if his point value is less than his opponent's. If not, or if the values are equal, opponent wins and receives a 10-point bonus in addition to the point score.

CONTRACT GIN RUMMY

Contract Gin Rummy is an entirely new game, combining some of the principles of contract bridge with the place and gambling element of ordinary gin rummy.

In the interest of avoiding serious mayhem, it is suggested that all hands study the rules below, before dealing:

STEP 1 – SEATING
As in bridge, partners sit opposite each other. In the ensuing explanation use this chart as your guide and consider yourself as 'A' – your partner thus being 'C'.

(A)

(D)   (B)

(C)

STEP II – DEALING
The dealer is determined by high cut. Let us assume that 'A' has won the deal:

(a) He deals ten cards to each player including himself.

(b) He places the remaining cards, of which there are twelve, face down in centre of table.

STEP III – EVALUATING YOUR HAND
Each player arranges his ten cards, as in ordinary gin rummy, by placing the sequences, the threes of a kind, and the 'possibilities' together. Everyone is now in position to evaluate his hand for purposes of bidding.

STEP IV – BIDDING

Bidding is based on the player's forecast of how many cards he thinks he will have to draw from the centre of the table in order to 'knock' with ten or less. The maximum bid is ten, and the minimum bid is obviously one. If a player thinks his hand is so poor it will take more than ten draws for him to 'knock' he may pass. Bidding procedure follows:

(a) The dealer is first to bid.

(b) Each player is only allowed two bids before the bidding closes.

(c) A double or a redouble is counted as a free bid.

(d) Bids from 10 through 6 receive smaller bonuses and smaller penalties than bids of 5 through 1 (consult the score chart on pages 155–6 for the actual count).

(e) In the first round of bidding it usually is best to make as high a bid as possible. A high bid means a bid which allows the bidder the maximum draws up to 10. There may be instances, however, where a player's hand may be so good that he may immediately want to shut out all other bidding with, say, a 5 bid. This would be considered a low opening bid and only an exceptional hand would justify such an opening.

(f) After the first bid is in, each succeeding bid must be lower than the previous one.

(g) Bidding proceeds to the left as in bridge.

(h) The bidder making the lowest bid wins the bid and his partner becomes the dummy.

STEP V – THE DUMMY

(a) After his partner has won the bid, the dummy must shuffle his cards so that he disarranges their order. He then places them face down on the table.

(b) Assuming, as an example, that 'A' has won the bid, 'C' consequently being the dummy, follows step (a) as above. Player 'A' then proceeds to discard any number of cards in his hand which he thinks weakens it.

(c) He places his discards in the centre of the table on the top of the twelve cards left over from the deal.

(d) He now proceeds to pick blindly from the dummy's hand the same number of cards he has discarded. In this way he may either strengthen or further weaken his hand by adding other unwanted cards. That is his gamble.

(e) After he has done this, he places the balance of the dummy's hand in the centre of the table and mixes it in with the twelve original cards and bidder's discards.

(f) The dummy may at this point sit beside his partner and inform him of the remaining cards that were in his hand. He may also assist in playing the game.

STEP VI – THE PLAY

(a) The bidder, player 'A', turns over the top card in the centre of the table as in gin rummy.

(b) That is all 'A' does. It is now 'B's' turn. If he cannot use this face-up card, 'B' must give his partner 'D' a chance either to accept or reject it before he may draw a down card from the pack. If 'D' accepts the card, then 'B' draws a card and makes his regular discard. Since 'D' and 'B' are partners, it would be to 'B's' interest to discard what he thinks would be helpful to 'D'.

(c) It is now 'D's' turn (remember that 'C; is the dummy and no longer in the playing of the game) either to accept or refuse the face-up discard.

(d) If he refuses it, he must ask 'A' if 'A' wishes it before he can draw another card. If 'A' should accept it 'D' loses his turn.

STEP VII – FORCING A LOSE

It will readily be seen from the above that it is possible to cause a player to lose a turn by accepting a discard which he has refused. It is naturally to the interest of the two players who are playing against the bidder to force him to lose his turn at drawing. Since he has contracted to draw a minimum number of cards in order to make his bid, he will obviously have great difficulty in making his contract if he is forced to lose many successive turns. Thus it would be to 'D's' advantage to make a discard which he is quite certain 'A' cannot use. And in most cases it would be advisable for 'B' to take his partner's discards even though they may not fit into his hand at all, in order for 'A' to lose his turn. Forcing lose is the most important manoeuvre in Contract Gin Rummy.

STEP VIII – SCORING

(a) If player 'A' 'knocks' and melds his hand, his opponents may discard on his hand as in regular gin. If he gins they may not.

(b) Assuming that 'A' knocks', his partial score, as in gin rummy, is the total of all the unmatched points held by both opponents, less of course, his own unmatched points.

(c) To this partial score he adds the bonus earned. (See below.)

(d) A game consists of 200 points – in other words, exactly double ordinary gin.

(e) Twenty points is counted for each box.

(f) A bonus of 100 points is given the winning couple.

(g) A 'schneider' or 'blitz' (a game which is won by a shut-out) counts for double the total.

CONTRACT GIN SCORE CHART

	1-5 bid	6-10 bid
BONUS POINTS TO BE ADDED TO GIN SCORE		
1. Bidder makes bid	20	10
2. Every play under bid	3	1
3. If doubled, then every play under bid	6	3
4. If doubled and makes bid	40	20

PENALTY POINTS TO BE ADDED TO OPPONENT'S GIN SCORE

1. Bidder fails to make bid	0	0
2. Every play over bid	3	1
3. If doubled, then every play over bid	6	3
4. If doubled, and bidder fails to make bid	20	10
5. Bidder loses hand	20	10
6. If doubled, and bidder loses hand	40	20

DEMONSTRATION GAME

(In following the steps of this demonstration game, refer to seating chart at the beginning.)

(1)   Assume 'A' is the dealer.

(2)   'A' opens the bidding with a bid of ten.

(3)   'B' has a very weak hand and passes.

(4)   'C' has a good hand and bids nine, thus underbidding his partner's hand to show strength and perhaps wishing to play the hand himself.

(5)   'D' bids eight.

(6)   'A; realises that this is his last chance to bid. he therefore bids his minimum – six.

(7)   'B' passes.

(8)   'C' passes.

(9)   'D passes.

(10) 'C' becomes the dummy and 'A' plays the hand.

(11) 'A' now discards three weak cards from his hand and picks, blindly, three cards from his partner's hand.

(12) The playing of the hand now begins with the bidder, 'A', who turns up the first card from the stock in the middle.

(13) 'A' improved his hand with the three cards he drew from the dummy and, after the fourth draw, he 'knocks' with four unmatched points in his hand. He catches 'B' with nineteen points and 'D' with fifteen points.

(14) Subtracting four points (his unmatched cards) from both 'B' and 'D's' score, he receives a total of twenty-six points.

(15) To this he adds ten points, the bonus for making the bid, and two additional points – one point each for every play under his bid of six.

(16) Thus, the total score for partners 'A' and 'C' is thirty-eight.

If bidder 'A' had been doubled, the scoring would have been as follows: 'A' would have received the regular twenty-six points as in the previous example from the unmatched cards in his opponent's hand. In addition to this, he would receive twenty points for being doubled and making his bid, and three points each for every play under his bid, which would make six additional points. His and his partner's total score, therefore, would be fifty-two points.

CANASTA

by Albert A. Ostrow

Canasta is a rummy game of Argentinian (some say Uruguayan) origin. It has been touted as the hottest thing in card games since gin and the best partnership game ever. Its publicists and enthusiasts claim it will decimate the ranks of bridge players, convert pinochlers and bewitch poker hounds. Time will tell.

You play the game with a double deck of cards shuffled together and hopped up with four jokers. With the deuces wild you have 12 wild cards in the playing pack of 108 cards.

From two to six people can take part but the game has better proportions when played two-handed or four-handed. Four-handed Canasta is played in partnerships and is definitely the most enjoyable form of the game.

A description follows according to the rules most generally played at the present. But it's no crime to stick in variations to suit the taste of your own circle.

THE DEAL: In the four-handed game players each get 11 cards in the deal, the rest of the pack going face down in the centre of the table as the stock. The top card is turned up to start a discard pile, technically known as 'the pack' but more often called 'the pot'. All cards that go into the discard pile are face up. The discard pile is kept squared.

If the first card faced is a wild card or a trey in the red suits, it is covered with another card from the stock. At the beginning, the discard pile must show a card that is not wild or a red three.

RED THREES: Red threes have a bonus value for or against your side. If you have been dealt one or more red threes originally, you place all such face up on the table when your turn to play comes and you restore your hand from the stock in the amount of threes you've put down.

A variation has all players immediately put down their red threes and the dealer replenish their hands from the stock before play begins. If you draw a red three during the play you face it on the table and take another card from the stock. If it comes to you as part of the pot, you must face it but you do not draw a card to replace it.

CANASTA ANGLES: The object, as in other rummy games, is to build melds. But Canasta melds are restricted to sets. Runs or sequences are not melds. You can meld or build on melds of three or four of a kind using natural or wild cards or both. In a meld of only three cards, two of them must be natural. In any case, you may not use more than three wild cards in a meld of seven cards of less.

A variation permits melds of sequences of three or more cards in the same suit.

Cards have a point count as follows: Joker, 50; deuce, 20; ace, 20; king down through the eight-spot, 10; cards below the eight (except deuces and red threes), 5.

The main idea is not to match up your hand quickly as in gin and knock but to build up canastas. There are melds of seven or more cards of the same rank and have a high bonus count. The bonus for going out in Canasta is small compared to the premiums for forming canastas.

To build up canastas you may start on any base meld of three cards and add more cards of the same rank as you go along in the play. No more than three wild cards may be used in building a canasta but once it has been completed you may add wild cards, or natural cards to it in any number you please.

Any melds you show on the table when play ends counts for your side. Cards left in your hand are deducted from your score according to their point count.

All of a side's melds are kept in front of one of the partners. You may add to any melds belonging to your side regardless of who started them. You make as many melds in your turn of play as you like. But you may not lay off on opponents' melds.

THE PLAY: First turn to play goes to the player at dealer's left. After that the play goes in continuous rotation.

In your turn you may always draw the top card of the stock. But the alternate play of taking the top card of the discard pile may be made only if one of your side has laid down a meld or melds having a point count of 5 points or more, known as the 'initial' or 'opening meld'. The opening meld must always be the first meld for your side.

(In later stages of the game the minimum count for your opening meld rises. See VULNERABILITY)

You establish your right to the top discard by melding with it at least two natural cards of the same rank from your hand, or a natural card of the same rank plus a wild card. You are also entitled to use the top discard (once your side has made an opening meld) if it can be added to a meld of the partnership showing on the table.

Any time you use the top discard you must take all the other cards of the pot into your hand. You may now use any of the other cards in the pot to form new melds or add to table melds. Taking the pot is an advantage in Canasta since the more cards you have the more melds you can make.

If your side has not made an opening meld you may take the top discard, provided you can show two natural cards to meld with it and provided you can produce sufficient additional meld or melds from your hand to give you the count for an opening meld. **You may not use any cards in the pot underneath the top discard to make up your opening meld.**

A turn of plays goes as follows: (1) Draw a card from the stock or take the top; (2) make a melding play or not as you choose; (3) make a discard.

PRIZE POTS: When there is a red three or wild card in the pot it is known as a prize pot. According to the rules most generally played at present you may not take a prize pot, even though your side has made an opening meld, unless you have two natural cards to match the top discard. (In a variation also played you may take any pot, prize or not, with only one natural card and a wild card.)

Deliberately discarding a wild card into the pot is part of the strategy of the game.

BLACK THREES: Black threes are blocking cards. That is, you may not take a discard pile topped by a black three even though you can match it with black threes from your hand. Black threes may not be melded except if doing so enables you to go out. (A variation permits you to meld black threes at any time or to a discard pile topped by one.)

ENDING THE HAND: When your side has completed at least one canasta, and not before then, you may go out by melding your remaining cards with or without a discard. Without a canasta you are required to retain at least one card in your hand.

Before you make any melding plays in your turn of play you may ask your partner, 'May I go out?'. You are bound by your partner's response. But you can go out without asking partner's permission.

IF THE STOCK RUNS OUT: When there are no more cards in the stock, play ends, except if the player whose turn it is after the last card has been drawn can use the top discard on any of the melds belonging to his side. In that case he is required to take it (and the pot). Play continues so long as the player whose turn it is can use the top discard on a table meld. This is known as being 'forced'.

When a player has not been forced and chooses not to take the top discard the hand ends.

SCORING: There is a 100 point bonus for melding out before the stock is gone; no bonus when it is gone. An additional 100 point bonus is scored for going out concealed, that is without having made a meld previously.

Both sides score 100 points for each red three on the table and 800 points for all four. But you lose 100 points per each red three if your side failed to make an opening meld.

Canastas without wild cards carry a bonus of 500; wild canastas score only 300.

All cards melded on the table (including the ones in canastas) are credited to your score according to their count. All cards remaining in the hand at the end of play are subtracted from your score; a red three in the hand carries a penalty of minus 500.

Both sides receive a net score on each deal and a cumulative running score is kept. First to reach 5,000 wins by the difference of the two scores. If both sides reach 5,000 in the same deal, the higher total wins.

VULNERABILITY: Until your side has a score of 1,500 your opening meld must have a count of at least 50. At 1,500 the required minimum is 90, and at 3,000 it is 120.

FOR TWO, THREE, FIVE OR SIX HANDS

In a two-handed game each player receives 15 cards and the popular requirement is two canastas to go out. In three-handed each one receives 13 cards and plays and scores for himself. In six-handed, three play as partners against three, sitting alternately. Three decks may be used in which case players receive 13 cards, game is 10,000 and two canastas are required to go out.

DEALER'S CHOICE

by Winston Hibler

The great American game of Poker is played by everyone from old-maid aunts in the front parlour to the boys in the back room. Several million players prefer the game 'Dealer's Choice' to straight Stud, so for those dealers who like to name their own poison, here are 18 games of 'Dealer's Choice' as compiled for an Esquire article by Winston Hibler:

FIVE-CARD STUD WITH THE HOLE CARD WILD

Deal it and bet it like straight Stud. Here's the twist – your hole card is wild and all like it in your hand. If you have a five in the hole, and a five and an ace up, you have Three Aces and they should win, but Doc may have made his Straight, so take it easy.

ROLL-EM

Another five-card Stud game. Two cards are dealt, face down, to each player who turns up whichever one he chooses and high hand bets. Each card, thereafter, is dealt face down, and each is bet before the next card is dealt. The player may turn up his hole card or the one he has just received, but he must, of course, always have one card in the hole. What usually wins it? Well, what wins at Stud? It's the same thing.

ROLL 'EM, HOLE CARD WILD

This one is a beaut, and you had better call in a C.P.A. to figure out your hand for you when the last card is dealt. Deal it the same as Roll 'em, but remember that the card you choose to keep in the hole is wild and all like it; so if you have two aces, turn one up and keep the other down in order that you may have two wild cards with which to work. If you catch another pair you will have Four of a Kind, or your wild cards will fit into a Straight or a Flush. If, however, you don't improve when your last card is dealt, turn up your other ace to make you Three Aces. A Flush or a Straight usually wins it, but the Three Aces will stand up once in a while.

BET OR GET OUT

Five cards in all. One card is dealt each player, face down. The player to the left of the dealer starts the betting each time a card is dealt. All five cards are dealt face down, and no player may check, he must either bet or get out. You may play this game with the deuces wild, or the treys, or the tens, or what-ever your favourite wild card happens to be, but it is really a better game just as it is.

NO PEEK

Five cards are dealt, face down, to each player and no bet is made until each has his five cards. No player is allowed to look at his hand, and if he does so, his hand is dead and he forfeits any right to the pot. The player to the left of the dealer turns one card and bets or checks. If he bets, all players wishing to remain in the pot must call. The next player to the left then turns his cards until he has topped the hand to his right but if he turns an additional card when he has already beaten the hand ahead of him, then his hand is dead. As

soon as a player beat the hand to his right he bets and all must call if they
wish to see their hands. As soon as any hand is raised out or drops out, the
high hand may bet again. The betting and turning goes on until all the
hands are turned or the players forced out. Same hands win as in Stud.

Here are some of the twists that can be given to Draw Poker:

ACES OR BETTER

This is simply Draw Poker with the exception that it takes Aces or better to
open. It is designed primarily to build up bigger and better pots. If no one
has Openers on the first round, the same dealer deals again and everyone
antes. The next round it takes Kings or better, and so on down to Jacks and
then up again until some player has the required Openers. It has never been
explained why all the players do not ante more in the first place, open on
Jacks and have it over with; but there it is, take it or leave it.

LEGS

Again this is straight draw with nothing wild, but this time the pot stays on
the table until any one player has won it twice, then it is won for 'keeps'.
And here's a warning: Don't play this one near quitting time, for it may be
well into the wee hours before one player does win twice.

PIG

A combination of Stud and Draw. Three cards are dealt to each player and
the player to the left of the dealer bets on his three cards; after the betting is
complete, another card is dealt and that is bet; then another. You have five
cards now, haven't you? All right, play it out as you would in Draw by discarding and drawing to your hand. Any pair opens, or you can open on
'your hat'. The game is a bit more interesting, incidentally, when played with
wild cards.

Here's what can be done with the game the Old Timers used to call
'Whisky Poker'.

DIZZY LIZ

Five cards are dealt to each player and four to the centre of the table. It takes
Jacks or better to open. When the pot has been opened and the betting complete, one of the centre cards is turned and the betting starts again; and so on
until all of the four cards in the centre are face up. The player who makes the
best hand with his five cards and the four in the centre is the winner. The
cards in the centre are not wild; they simply play as part of each player's
hand.

CALIFORNIA

The same as Dizzy Liz except that five cards are dealt to the centre and one
turned up as a starter before the betting begins. No openers are required,
and the player to the left of the dealer starts it off by betting or checking. In

[162]

these last two games a Full House is usually the hand that wins it; so if you are sitting there with two pairs, stop yelling for someone to go out and mix a round of drinks – do it yourself and save money.

OMAHA

Still another version of the above; but just to make it wilder than it is, the dealer puts a chip on one of the cards that is face down in the centre, which when it is turned up is wild and all like it. Some fun, but you better have Four Aces or a Straight Flush when that last card is turned.

There are perhaps half-a-dozen other versions of Dizzy Liz, but your imagination is as good as anyone else's, so see what you can do, using the above games as a foundation.

Now to the pot-builders. The various forms of the famous old Seven-Toed Pete are becoming more and more popular. More cards on which to bet, and so more money in the pot.

BASEBALL

Deal it like Seven-card Stud with the first two and the last card dealt face down. The nines are wild; the four spot dealt face up to a player gives him an extra card; a three spot strikes him out, and out he goes – no matter how much he has invested in the pot.

The player who has a four spot up receives his extra card usually after all of the other players have been dealt their card for that round. A three or a four spot in the hole plays as any other card in the hand. The betting is the same as in any Stud game; the first three cards are bet and every round thereafter. It usually takes a Full House to win this one, but a Flush will stand up now and then.

ONE-EYED JACKS

Seven-card Stud with the two one-eyed Jacks wild.

5 AND 10

Seven-card Stud with the fives and tens wild. But you must have at least one of each. In other words, if your first three cards are fives, you have three fives and nothing more; but if you should happen to catch a ten on one of the next four cards it will give you four wild cards. Deuces and treys are sometimes substituted for the fives and tens. With less than Four of a Kind in this, you're not interested.

LOW HOLE

Seven-card Stud with the lowest card in the hole wild and all like it. The last card which is dealt to the player face down usually makes or breaks the hand.

Look...if you have two fours in the hole and two Jacks face up, you have Four Jacks; but if you should be so unfortunate as to catch a trey on that last down card, then your lowest card in the hole is a trey and you have a Full

House, and no more. Anything can happen in this game, so look for Royal Flushes and Fives of a Kind.

444

Four down, four up, and the fours are wild. Bet on the first four cards and on each card thereafter. Fold up with less than a high Full House.

333

Three down, three up and the threes are wild. Bet on the first three cards and on each card thereafter. A Straight or better should take the money.

HIGH-LOW

This variety is applied to the straight versions of Stud and Draw; it is just another form of the time-honoured Low Ball. The player plays his hand for either high or low, but does not have to announce which way he is playing it until the last card is dealt. The highest and the lowest hands split the pot. Ace is always high and cannot be used as a low card except as part of a Straight in the high hand.

PLAYING POKER TO WIN

by George F. Browne

The most difficult point to master in the art of poker is the fine science of quitting. Especially when the cards are running right for it takes a foxlike cunning to sense precisely when they'll peter out.

This lack of perception accounts in a large measure for the high mortality among 'luck' players. Scudding along under a stiff breeze they blandly ignore squalls ahead. So reach for your hat and hit the deck if the high tide you've been riding slowly begins to ebb. The crest of your wave has been reached and the breakers, if disregarded, will shower you with regrets. On second thought, since bidding the shorn lambs a cheerful adieu hardly seems cricket, it might be best to master a subtler technique for clinging to the booty.

The bright thing to do, then, is to drop out of active competition until the cards start rolling your way for the long shots, until now completed with ease, will soon bog down like an Italian blitzkrieg. Consummate artistry should be used so the hedge is not apparent and chips previously flung about with plutocratic abandon should be doled out with artistic finesse. Lay back and ride along, for a tight play now will show a profit when taps are sounded.

'But if you want a really unbeatable combination', argue the experts, 'this style of play will have to be combined with a mastery of mathematical probabilities.'

And at that there must be something to this mathematical angle, for Johnny MacGregor, as canny a Scot as ever mickeyfinned a jack-pot, is one of its most rabid enthusiasts. And although the game's a hobby with him, it's a pasteboard gold mine, simply because he's a specialist at mathematically booting a minor hand into a major victory.

'Among the uninitiated', says Mac, 'the fall of cards is supposed to be controlled by the fickle goddess 'Chance'. What they don't know is that a good many years ago skeptical mathematicians embalmed this erratic jade and dug up the laws of probabilities; laws which discount chance entirely. Mathematical patterns must exist in all things, poker included, and cards honestly shuffled must fall with a relative frequency. Their progression is an unchanging as the days of the week, the fall of the tides or the path of the sun.'

And therein, wrapped up and ready for delivery, lies the meat of the MacGregor Equation. Not a parcel of thinly sliced baloney but porterhouse steaks of wisdom from a master strategist whose successful manoeuvres will put chips in your corner and logic in your play.

For this is no theoretical musing. Experiments show, and you don't have to take his word for it (try it yourself), that in each thousand deals the following hands will appear.

No rank	503 times
One pair	422 times
Two pairs	47 times
Triplets	21 times
Straights	3 times
Flushes	2 times
Total	998

The other two hands will contain either full house, fours or straight flushes.

But of that, more later. The first thing to bear in mind at the next weekly session is that the deck contains 2,598,960 poker hands. Only one of these can be dealt to you. So finding a gold mine in Central Park will be a lot easier than annexing that Royal Flush you've been yearning for. Hope, however, springs eternal but since dreams must be shattered let's start the blasting by figuring your exact chance of getting an unbeatable combination on the deal.

The only unbeatable hand is straight poker is, of course, the straight flush. Using a full deck (52 cards), there are ten possible straight flushes in each suit; in the four suits, forty. These highly profitable nuggets nestle snugly somewhere in the 2,598,960 hands the deck provides. Since only forty straight flushes are available, and since any of the other combinations may turn up, your chance of jarring a straight flush loose is confined to one-fortieth of the total combinations. You have therefore 64,974 possibilities. However, receiving only one hand, you have only one chance of success, while stacked against you are 64,973 chances of failure. The odds against snaring a straight flush on the deal, therefore is 64,973 to 1. This includes the four Royal Flushes.

The odds against getting any other combination on the deal can be arrived at by the same process. Unless you have a flair for figures you won't care to figure them out. Anyway the table following will save you the trouble. The first column shows the number of combinations of each type in the deck.

ODDS AGAINST HOLDING VARIOUS HANDS ON THE DEAL

QUANTITY	HAND	ODDS AGAINST
40	Straight Flush	64,973 to 1
624	Four of a kind	4,164 to 1
3,744	Full house	693 to 1
5,108	Flush	508 to 1
10,200	Straight	254 to 1
54,912	Triplets	46 to 1
123,552	Two pairs	20 to 1
1,098,240	One pair	$1\frac{1}{4}$ to 1
1,302,540	No pair	EVEN
2,598,960		

If you have looked at the table you will note an almost even chance of getting a pair on the deal. But even a pair has its advantages when its mathematical possibilities of improvement are known. It shouldn't be sneered at for it improves, if high enough, to a 3 to 2 winner over a two-pair entry.

This is not guesswork. It's the mathematical certainty of the unchangeable laws of probabilities. As MacGregor says, 'The improvement of any hand depends entirely on the undeviating pattern in which cards fall'. This pattern can be dissected, translated into figures and the odds against improvement of any hand calculated. However, the process is tedious and involved so a ready reference table showing the odds against improvement has been set up below.

A daily workout with this table should sharpen your playing, put a razor edge on your technique and account for many scalps heretofore immune.

ORIGINAL HAND	CARDS DRAWN	IMPROVED HAND	ODDS AGAINST
One pair	3	Two pairs	5.25 to 1
	3	Triplets	8 to 1
	3	Full house	97 to 1
	3	Fours	359 to 1
	3	Any improvement	2.5 to 1
Two pairs	1	Full house	11 to 1
Triplets	2	Full house	15.5 to 1
	2	Fours	22.5 to 1
Four straight (open ends)	1	Straight	5 to 1
Four straight (interior)	1	Straight	11 to 1
Four-flush	1	Flush	4.5 to 1
Three-flush	2	Flush	23 to 1
Two-flush	3	Flush	96 to 1
Pair with odd Ace	2	Two pair Ace high	8 to 1
	2	Triplets	12 to 1
Ace	4	One pair	4 to 1
	4	Two more Aces	63 to 1
Ace and King	3	Either paired	3 to 1

Now to get back to MacGregor's strategy. When holding two pairs, if you are sure you are fighting triplets, your best line of defence is to throw away the smaller pair, when lower than tens, and buy three cards.

The advantage of holding an ace kicker with a pair is a perennial argument. But not from the standpoint of its mathematical probabilities of improvement. Some players are for it, some agin it. Confidentially, it smells. It is true that when holding the kicker the probability of ending up with two pairs is slightly better than when holding the pair alone. This advantage is more than offset, however, by the probability on the pair to improve to triplets, a full house or fours. The odds are as follows:

ORIGINAL HAND	CARDS DRAWN	IMPROVED HAND	ODDS AGAINST
One pair	3	Two pairs	5.25 to 1
One pair	3	Triplets	8 to 1
One pair	3	Full House	97 to 1
One pair	3	Fours	359 to 1

[167]

One pair plus kicker	2	Two Pairs	5 to 1
One pair plus kicker	2	Triplets	12 to 1
One pair plus kicker	2	Full house	119 to 1
One pair plus kicker	2	Fours	1,080 to 1

After taking a look at the table you won't need the MacGregor equation to tell you to heave that kicker you've been holding into the ashcan.

And believe you me, there's dynamite in pairs. Especially when a high pair or a small two-pair hand gets caught in a crowd of them.

To convince yourself of this, deal out four hands containing respectively a pair of aces, a pair of sevens, and a pair of jacks. The remaining hand can hold a pair of sixes and tens. Or, if you prefer, use pairs of your own choice. The object, for purposes of comparison of the effective value of a crowd of pairs, is to have one fairly low pair, one intermediate pair and one high pair; plus one low two-pair hand.

When this has been done, have each of the pairs discard and draw three cards while the two-pair hand discards and draws one. In the majority of the cases you will find that the low of the intermediate hand has improved over the high pair, or the two-pair hand. The reason for this becomes clear when consideration is given to the fact that the low and intermediate pair hands have two opportunities for improvement as against the high pair's one. Also there are three opportunities for improvement of all the pairs against the two-pair's one.

As a matter of fact, the small two-pair hand misses the bus, seven out of ten times. In a battle against three one-pair hands, one of the singles after the draw will hold two pairs half of the time and one of them will hold threes, one-third of the time. The small two-pair hand catches the bus in less than one out of three tries.

When holding threes, it is well to inveigle small pairs in, so do not frighten them off with a raise before the draw. On the other hand, when holding a pair of aces, shake off the small fry by a raise. Before doing so, however, be careful to see that no two-pair hand is around, otherwise you'll do his dirty work and in addition may have to battle him alone and unaided.

In considering a raise, be governed by the strategy to be employed. To frighten out weak hands that lose often and require a large profit for the risk they are taking, raise to the limit. To keep hands in, take it easy, for you want to see lots of weak hands around. In this event a moderate raise will do. After the draw, you can let loose. The pot is then bigger, weak hands that have improved will mistakenly attempt to protect their investment, and your chances of being seen are proportionately greater.

While you may not be out for a killing, you certainly want to draw blood, so extreme care should be used in opening. Your chances of being squelched in a seven-handed game are lessened if you open only with a pair of kings or better; a six-handed game, queens; a five-handed game, jacks. If one of seven players before you passes, try considering it a six-handed game and open with queens; a five-handed game if two pass and open with jacks. Quite a few of your entries may be lost in this manner, but that will be overcome later, for players who have won several pots on your entries are inclined to come in readily when you open.

Bluffing is an art which, unless you are a master strategist, you should rarely indulge. The bluff of threes is the most successful. In this, imitate a normal two-pair hand. Raise to the limit before the draw and buy only one card. See a raise after buying, or better it, and you will probably corral the pot. This trick also confuses your opponents who, when sizing you up for two pairs, can never be sure they are right. A good rule is to play a third of your threes that way.

Play a pair of aces, once in a while, as you would threes. Raise moderately and buy two cards. Also play two pairs occasionally as you would a pat hand. While the latter dodge will not always deceive the wiseacres it will chase some of the dangerous one-pair hands to cover. This is the easiest bluff to carry, as the only stratagem required is to raise to the limit before the draw, nonchalantly waive aside the proffered cards and wait for the fadeout. For this bluff the choice position is next to the dealer. Be careful not to overdo this, for a pat hand should show up no more than seven times in a thousand deals, and a pat hand oftener than that may justly be suspected of bluffing. Reducing the margin, a pat hand shows up in a seven-handed game once in twenty rounds, and in a five-handed game once in twenty-eight rounds. The odds are about five to two in a pat hand that a straight or a flush has been dealt.

The equation says that a good time to pull up stakes or lay low is during a steady losing streak. Believe it, please. While you may not want to leave the game, don't become discouraged and desperate. Forcing brings nothing except additional losses. Play carefully and coolly. Wait till you get decent cards before going to town and, by all that's holy, lay off the long shots. Take a walk to the washroom, it kills sluggishness and revives wilted energy.

A certain rhythm in which he repeats himself is subconsciously employed by each player. The pattern of this melody in your opponents should be carefully studied, and, with experience, you will almost always be able to tell what will be done in any situation. And now, if you can't win with all this information, I'd suggest you stop playing cards. I have.

BLUFFING AT BRIDGE

by Hart Stilwell

The time comes in the life of every bridge player when he get sick and tired of following suit to the opponent's high cards, and finds that he has, without any visible explanation of logic, indulged in a remarkable bid.

Perhaps he feels that it will change his luck. I knew a player who held stubbornly to this theory. When I was his partner I was always on the look-out for an earth-shaking bid, based on a few tens and eights, after a protract-ed session of worthless hands. I was seldom disappointed.

'I got sick of following suit', he would explain after we had gone down a few thousand points. 'Thought maybe I would change our luck.'

Of course when the opponents got through with his bid it was usually too late for a change of luck to do him, or me either, much good. But at any rate, he had broken the monotony of following suit, for it seems that when a man starts getting a run of worthless hands, the distribution is usually 4-3-3-3.

Sometimes I believe his idea is not so bad. I know that every man who plays bridge is likewise tempted on occasions, but few yield to the tempta-tion. There is a modest tingling of pleasure from suddenly calling out 'four spades' when you have nothing higher than jack or queen. You are flinging a challenge into the teeth of fate.

Some of these bids have met disaster. Most of them have. Those I manage to forget in a hurry. No man enjoys remembering the time he went down

[180]

six, doubled and redoubled, and I say redoubled for a man's partner usually has a nasty habit of redoubling on such occasions.

But when the screwball bids pay off, then I love to linger over them on the quiet afternoon months or even years later, playing the hand over once more, watching the look of astonishment on the faces of the enemy as their aces and kings are ruffed away, and gloating once more over that overtrick which was the crowning insult of all.

I am gloating right now over just such a hand. I had been meekly following suit until it began to lose interest. Any hand I picked up with a king in it began to look big, and I felt a strong desire to bid welling up within me. My partner must have realised this, for he sat there in stony silence when I was doubled, when he had sound reason to redouble if my bid had been based on anything near the values that it indicated. In fact, his thinking was even worse than that, for later he confessed to me that he was contemplating going to a small slam. I still shudder when I think or it.

I sat South, then, and drew this mess of pottage:

		North	
		S – Axx	
		H – KQJxx	
West		D – xx	East
S – Qx		C – Kxx	S – K
H – xxx			H – Axxxx
D – QJxxx			D – AKxx
C – xxx			C – Axx
		South	
		S – Jxxxxxx	
		H – none	
		D – xx	
		C – QJxx	

The gentleman on my right, East, dealt and opened one heart. He had been doing it all evening. The only time there was any variation was when he opened one spade instead of one heart. I don't think I had played a hand in fourteen hands. When I did get some face cards they were clubs, and I was always outbid. When I finally work out my own system of bridge, there are going to be no clubs in the deck – just a few extra spades and hearts. They are the cards to hold.

So I figured it was time I played a hand. Holding this pile of junk I bid four spades at once, before I had time to reflect on the complete lack of logic in the bid. I realised that even a modest amount of thought on the matter would have resulted in a pass, so I was careful not to indulge in this thought.

This four–spade bid rode all the way back to East, and after a casual glance at his ace and kings, and knowing full well that I was in a humour to make a bid regardless of what I held, he doubled.

When it arrived back at my partner he started studying his hand, and no matter how hard I looked at him he kept right on studying it and wouldn't pass. Finally, when I was on the verge of shouting at him to go ahead and pass, he did pass. I eased back in my chair, figuring I would no more than nine hundred or eleven hundred points, since we weren't vulnerable. I figured it was a cinch to take at least four of my spades, and I might even take a club – who knows.

Well the opening heart lead brought down the dummy and a shower of delight with it. The spectacle of that dummy, with a heart lead through it, was worth all the bad sets I had suffered in three or four months.

And what followed was worth twice as much.

I put up the king which brought out the ace which was ruffed.

I played over to the ace of spades, got rid of my diamonds on the queen and jack of hearts, which was perfectly safe since the queen was the outstanding trump and it was high. Then I made the enemy a present of the ace of clubs and the high trump, thus making the doggone bid with an overtrick.

East got up and put on his hat and walked away. I haven't seen him since then, and sometimes I worry about him, for as he went out the door he was muttering. 'No man objects to losing at bridge, but to sit at the same table with anybody fool enough to bid four spades on that hand and lucky enough to make five...'

That was a noble incident in my bridge career.

I recall another flurry into the realm of the fantastic that has given me much to gloat over. We were so far behind that anything might happen. It did.

I dealt and again sat South, since nobody objected. I picked up the stack of junk shown in the South hand opposite:

```
                          North
                          S – Kxxx
                          H – AKxxxx
                          D – Ax
        West              C – x                    East
        S – QJxx                                   S – Axxxx
        H – none                                   H – xxx
        D – Jxxxxx                                 D – KQxx
        C – AJx                                    C – K
                          South
                          S – none
                          H – QJ10x
                          D – x
                          C – Qxxxxxxx
```

After a casual glance at my hand I opened with three clubs, in spite of the then current rule that to open with three in a minor suit you must have the top honours. West passed and my partner bid three hearts. East passed and I bid six hearts, on the theory that if my partner couldn't make it, he had no business bidding at all.

East opened the ace of spades and began abusing me for foolish bidding as I put down the hearts and clubs and the diamond. It always seems odd to me that people will berate you for making a bid which they expect to set. But when East started looking for Spades and couldn't find any, he stopped talking. My partner ruffed the spade ace and led a club. The rest of the tricks were in the bag – at least, we put them in the bag. If there was any way to defeat the contract, East and West never discovered it.

There are plenty of bridge players who might have opened three clubs on the hand. I am not proud of that bid at all. It's the six – heart bid that strikes my fancy. A man might even go back over the hand carefully and justify the six – heart bid. But I hope nobody does it. I love to feel that it was a pure venture into the unknown – and one that paid off nicely.

The interesting part of the hand to me is that six spades could have been made by the opponents.

I even derive a certain fiendish satisfaction from some screwball bids that have been set and set badly. For many is the time when a careful check afterward will reveal that I saved a thousand or so points by such a bid. I never fail to remind the opponents of this, which is another reason why I am extremely popular as a bridge player.

One such hand sticks in my crop, quite pleasantly, at the moment, and I reproduce it here in order to gloat over it a bit more. On this hand I sat North, my partner being a gentleman from South Carolina who flatly refused to occupy that position.

The hand follows:

```
                        North
                        S – xx
                        H – xxxxxxx
                        D – xxx
                        C – x

    West                                        East
    S – AJx                                     S – Kxxxx
    H – Q                                       H – AK
    D – AKQxx                                   D – Jxxx
    C – xxxx                                    C – AK

                        South
                        S – Qxx
                        H – Jxx
                        D – x
                        C – QJxxxx
```

You will note upon careful examination that I held what is known in the profession as a yarborough.

The gentleman on my right, West, dealt and bid one diamond.

Well, I didn't pass. I knew East for a malicious sort of fellow who could think of nothing more satisfying than setting somebody. What particularly delighted him was to hold the high cards in your trump suit and then double. Evidently he held them. At least I didn't.

So I decided to bid just enough to get doubled. I bid three hearts and East doubled. Thus the bidding ended.

Well, I went down, of course. I lost every trick it was possible to lose, I guess, going down for a penalty of five hundred. But the hand, and particularly my bidding, was an outstanding success. The vulnerable opponents had an iron clad cinch for six spades or seven diamonds, and could have made seven spades by finessing for the queen.

Certainly a small slam would have been bid, except for East's malicious yearning to see me squirm while he took the high trumps.

What irritated the enemy on this hand wasn't so much the points they lost. It was my bidding. They claimed that it was even dishonest and against the rules to bid three hearts holding no honour cards. Incidentally we won the rubber, which didn't make East and West feel any better.

Now I am not advising you to set out on a course of wild bidding on hands that are doomed. Such bidding would soon take the interest out of bridge, at least for your partner. I am merely pointing out that there are times when a thing can go just so far and then it not only ceases to be entertaining but it becomes a downright nuisance.

In times like that almost any kind of a diversion is likely to enliven the proceedings. When the diversion, in the form of a fantastic bid, plays off – then, brother, you've been through a real experience in bridge. You've got something sweet you can look back on.

ESQUIRE'S NEW
THREE-HANDED BRIDGE

Here's a streamlined version of Contract Bridge dreamed up by Squire Albert A. Ostrow for the Knights of the Square Table. This three–handed game of Contract with oomph, flashed into the mind of Mr. Ostrow one evening on the boring 5:38 local, and from that Bridge for Three reached its final shape...the perfect game for three marooned bridge hounds with no fourth in sight.

Deal four hands, one to each player, the left–over hand remaining face down. The dealer then opens with his bidding just as though he had a partner. The second hand may support this bid, overcall, or make an opening bid over a pass. The same goes for the third hand. If the third hand bids a suit already bid in partnership, he becomes the declarer. (That means that if the first bidder bids spades, either or both of the other two hands can raise in spades. If both so raise, however, the third hand becomes declarer.)

When the final contract is reached, declarer may choose any of the three hands for his dummy, regardless of previous bidding, raises, etc.; if he picks a partner hand, bonuses and overtricks are split. However, if he chooses the blind hand, he's rewarded will full bonuses.

In the event declarer elects to choose one of the two other players' hands as dummy, the remaining player plays with the blind hand, and the game resolves itself into the familiar pattern of Double–Dummy.

If, on the other hand, he chooses the blind hand, the other two players become defending partners and play proceeds exactly as in four–handed bridge.

There is a 300–point bonus for the game, with all overtricks as in the standard score, nonvulnerable Partials get a flat 50 points per man, regardless of the level of the bid. Penalties are the same as the regulation game, always nonvulnerable. When there are two defenders against a contract, penalties are split. If there is only one defender, he collects full penalties.

There are few rules, so as to keep the game as streamlined as possible, but these few additional are essential:

1. Declarer is barred from taking a doubling hand for his dummy.

2. An opening lead is barred from the blind hand. (This shuts out the possibility of a player seeing two hands before making his opening lead.)

3. If a third hand bids a suit already bid in partnership, he becomes the declarer.

Brain Teasers

1. BOOKWORM

Two books, Volumes 1 and 2, stand side by side in order from left to right on a bookshelf. Not including bindings, each book is one inch thick; the bindings are each an eighth of an inch thick. Starting from page one, Volume 1, a hungry bookworm eats its way to the last page of Volume 2. How many inches did he consume?

2. DOUBLING LILY

A circular pool, twenty-five feet in diameter, has a remarkable lily in its centre. This lily grows by doubling its area each day. At the end of thirty days, the lily exactly covers the pool. In how many days does this lily cover half the pool's area?

3. ROPE LADDER

An observant person noted a rope ladder dangling from a ship in a harbour, with its bottom six rungs underwater. Also, he saw that each rung was four inches wide and that the rungs were ten inches apart. If the tide rose at the rate of five inches per hour, how many rungs would be submerged in three hours?

4. FOREHEAD MARKS

Three men, A, B, and C, are tested for quick thinking. On the forehead of each a cross is marked which, they are told, may be either blue or white. They are then taken to an empty room. None of the three knows the colour of his own cross or is allowed to speak to the others, but each one is told he may leave the room if he either sees two white crosses or determines the colour of his own cross. A is a sharp fellow. He notes that both B and C have blue crosses, and after a few seconds of quick thinking, he leaves the room, having determined the colour of his own cross. What was the process by which he determined the answer, and what was the colour of his cross?

5. CIGARETTES

A cigarette fiend in Zion City was out of cigarettes - and you can't buy cigarettes in Zion City. Desperately he hunted through his hotel room, where he had been illegally smoking, and collected a total of thirty-six dead butts, too short to be smokeable. By experiment, however, he found that, with newspaper and ingenuity, he could make a more or less satisfactory cigarette out of every six butts. So he made and smoked as many cigarettes as he possibly could, at the rate of six butts per cigarette. How many did he smoke?

6. FOX, GOOSE AND CORN

A man has a fox, a goose and some corn. He must cross a river; however, he can take only one at a time. If he leaves the goose with the corn to take the fox over, the goose will devour the corn. If he leaves the fox alone with the goose, Reynard will devour the gander. How shall he get them all across?

7. HOCUS-POCUS

Here's a cryptarithm, which poses a problem in addition, subtraction, division or multiplication with letters instead of numbers. The object is to find the numbers. One problem I concocted was in addition, thus:

$$
\begin{array}{r}
H\ O\ C\ U\ S \\
P\ O\ C\ U\ S \\
\hline
P\ R\ E\ S\ T\ O
\end{array}
$$

Answers to Brain Teasers

1. The bookworm consumed only a quarter of an inch. When two volumes are in order from left to right on a bookshelf, the first page of Volume 1 and the last page of Volume 2 are separated only by the two covers.

2. Twenty-nine days.

3. Six rungs would still be submerged. The ship with the ladder rises with the tide, of course!

4. A's cross was blue. He figured it this way: If I were white, B would decide he is blue, for otherwise C would see two whites, and would leave the room. Likewise, C would know that he is blue or else B would have gone out. Since both of them stay in the room, I must be blue also.

5. Perhaps the cigarette problem is fair only for cigarette smokers, but that is a great majority of the literate population these days. The point to it is that the desperate smoker, having made and smoked the six cigarettes he can obviously manufacture out of collection of butts, will have six butts left from the new cigarettes. Out of those six new butts, he can make and smoke a seventh cigarette. Answer: seven. But don't let any disgruntled victim object that he still has a butt left at that point. The problem clearly states that it takes no less than six to make a smokeable cigarette.

6. Oh, yes, if you haven't solved the fox, goose, and corn problem, there are two ways of getting them across: He first takes the goose, returns and fetches the fox and takes back the goose. He leaves the goose at the starting point and takes over the corn, and then returns and fetches the goose. Or, for variety, he can take over the goose, return and fetch the corn, at which time he takes back the goose. Then he leaves the goose at the starting point and takes over the fox, after which he returns and fetches the goose.

7. The answer to HOCUS plus POCUS equals PRESTO is 92836 plus 12836 equals 105672.

After-dinner Witchcraft

If you would make a hit with the beautiful young ladies, don't step up to the piano, prattle on about Picasso or memorize the New York Times book reviews (let alone read a book itself). Turn on the mumbo-jumbo! Claim that you're a psychic and you're in – with fortune-telling for instance.

FORTUNE TELLING

Fortune-telling, especially by cards, consists mainly of unabashed, facile, and highly greased fibbing. Pre-information helps, too. If you are not a good liar, practice lying in secret; go up to your mirror and let forth such a flow of lies that even your reflection blanches and turns away its head in shameful meditation that it is your exact counterpart. Moreover you must learn to so go on that the fib-flow is never stopped. When you can do this well, you are prepared to take your first lessons in card-laying.

Presupposing that you have learned to lie well, you must now exert what is loosely known as 'hypnotic influence'; this is very easy as it consists mainly in astounding the 'subject' through telling him or her that which is most apparently obvious concerning himself.

People having their fortunes told are under a kind of hypnosis anyway and will believe almost anything you tell them. And it needs only a glance to see whether your stab into the psychic has reached home and if you have struck, then you are indeed in luck. One little strike and you may go ahead and foretell her practically anything.

It is always well to foretell that she is going to fall in love with a young man. If she presses you to add his description and you can think of no one else, describe yourself.

There are a number of manholes in fortune-telling, which it would be well to avoid. Remembering Rule No.1, of pre-information, and Rule No.2, of superlative lying, keep well in mind Rule No.3, which is, use no known system. If you lay down your cards in a known system this very system may be very well known to your frail victim, and should this be the very unfortunate case you will probably soon find a Ming vase wrapped around your broken neck. On the contrary, you must lay your cards down in a most complicated arrangement – any arrangement will do provided it is not an arrangement you have ever seen before. After you lay the cards down you will now spend a long time studying them – the longer the better – and as you crouch over each card, you will mumble 'Up-hump!' This signifies that

[178]

you getting a load of something pretty terrific and that you are endeavouring to piece this mess together although, apparently, you hate to do so. She will already be shaking in a quiver of apprehension.

And by now, Mr. Psychologist, tell her a nice, good, pleasant fortune. She will be so relieved that she will be very predisposed to believe anything you say, if you say it firmly.

To tell the actual fortune, first draw a long breath (this will send blood to your brain and oil up the muscles in your tongue) and then spiel. Pointing from one card to the other you will now proceed to deliver as brilliantly as you can, and Heaven help you if you stop. If you find that you can think at all, try to draw upon every piece of eavesdropping or pre-information that you can. Don't look closely at the cards; the less you know about them, the better. Guide yourself firmly but delicately by her ejaculations; you must constantly know whether you are upon the right trail and consequently be prepared in an instant to swerve if disaster appears imminent. When a trail is hot she will brighten with confidence. When it is cold she will look at you clammily through half-closed eyes.

Lets us suppose that early in the card-laying you have had the good fortune to stumble across a personage or situation which is obviously kosher and of the most tremendous interest to her. This incidentally is the most tremendous luck that can happen to any fortune teller. Not only can you now efficiently cook 'his' goose, but you can also safely begin to coax and prod the 'subject' with card after card – 'by the way this card would seem to mean…that is true, isn't it?' etc., etc. And you need not worry. By this time she will be so completely under the card-laying hypnosis, so utterly astonished that you should have turned up something of secret but sizzling importance to her, that she will now scarcely permit you to tell her fortune, but she will now proceed to tell it for you! In the remote future she will always believe quite absolutely that you have told her the very things she actually told you, and loudly indeed will she sing your praises! And now, if you are only the least tiny bit unscrupulous she will gladly come to hear you play Hindemith or to look at your priceless Picassos; why not cook her a Crêpe Suzette while you are about it?

But if you blush easily and are not a good liar, why not try table-tipping and have a table do your talking for you?

TABLE TIPPING

Table-tipping also has the advantage of being even more mesmeric than card-laying; the eerie atmosphere will not only set the lady's psychological tomtom beating, but it will also make her afraid to go home alone at night. You will now simply call loudly for a small table – if possible select one with one leg a little shorter than the others – then place four of five persons around the table and have everyone spread his hand out flat, thumbs touching each other and little finger tips touching the little fingers of the persons alongside. This is, you explain, to keep the "electrical body-fluid" unbroken and acting upon the table; this very favourable condition will lure sundry loose spirits to try their hands on an evening's terrestrial conversation. All spirits use the same code, a rather imbecile one; A is signalled by one rap, B I signalled by two, C is signalled by three, and so on down to Z (incidentally a rather tiresome letter to telegraph). But in table-tipping everybody has plenty of time, and no one seems to care if our first spirit telegraphs something like this 'WLEALKDLKJFADLKJFADLDL' for you can easily explain this as the work of either a malicious little spirit who always annoys you at first or the signal of an ancient Persian Prince who has never learned English but who has been trying all of these years to 'break though' without, however, any apparent success.

All is now ready except for the dimming of the lights and the placing of a scribe with paper and pencil at a far corner of the room. He will take down any possible messages. You are now able to proceed. With your hands upon the small table and after about three minutes of expectant waiting you will now exert a small pressure upon the rickety table causing it to move an inch or two along the floor. You know exclaim,

'There! Didn't you feel something? I felt something!'

The table moves again. You say with suppressed excitement, 'The spirit is approaching.'

Then the table begins to rap. (You are merely upsetting its small balance as rapidly and surely as a machine gun.) The short leg is jittering in code against the floor. 'I-I-I-I-I-I-I-I-I.' You now pretend to be angry with the spirit. 'What do you want?' you whisper hoarsely into the half-darkness.

IAMTHEDEADTRYINGTOGETMYMESSAGEITISOF
GREATESTEMPORTANCE

After the scribe has separated this into English, and it has made a certain disturbing impression, the table will move to a new section of the floor, twisting and turning en route. You all move your chairs with it and set up a new base of operations. It will now tap:

XYZLMNOPQRSTOOOOOOOOOOOOO

Now this you will have none of. You are severe. 'Malicious spirit leave us!

Let the friendly control break though!' Everybody shivers; the table com-
mences tapping again.

IAMDEADIAMDEADIAMDEADXY
QUTYSLEDXADKDDDXXXOOO

Again you have to pull the spirit back upon the track, but soon he will
really open up and give you all some pretty wonderful advice. If this advice
isn't of the kind that will make that lovely redhead on the other side of the
table sit up and resolve to make several important changes in her immediate
date book, then you should not be head man at a table-tipping party.

NUMEROLOGY

Numerology is another attractive parlor game and it will entice your beautiful victim to sit with you over a page of your pencilled numerals for hours
upon end. There is nothing to it. All that is necessary is for you to maintain
stoutly that you have an older and much more accurate system of
Numerology than any Numerology system ever discovered before, yours
having come directly from the ancient Chaldeans, whereas all alter systems
stem from the Phoenicians who had already fairly bungled it, so accounting
for the fact that so many people today having their numbers read are deeply
dissatisfied with the results thereof. This, you aver, could never happen with
your older and more perfect system.

You now write down the letters of her name and quickly, without apparently thought, mark a cipher – any cipher – underneath each letter. It matters not if you should accidentally have the same numeral under B and R…
your system is different, remember. You will now do an enormous amount
of multiplication, subtraction, and addition, and if you want, you can throw
in a little higher calculus just to impress. At least you are ready to tell her
fortune. Make it a good one.

(If you want to throw in a few remarks about her glandular personality at
this point you will give her that comfortable feeling that nothing can be concealed from you. She feels as if she were nude before you, incidentally an
extremely homelike and relaxing attitude. She will automatically think 'Oh
what's the use of resisting him, he can see right through me anyway.')

ASTROLOGY

But the really smart fortune teller will soon drop all these infantile pursuits and take up, instead, Astrology. Astrology is really the Big Noise follow-up of after-dinner witchcraft. The method is simplicity itself. Remember there are dozens of Astrology magazines upon the news stands containing exact information about the stars many years in advance. Therefore should you, at your dinner party, met the most attractive young girl you have ever seen, be sure to tell her fortune by one of the above methods, and if she is impressed, ask her for the date and hour of her birth. You will make a note of this and assure her that you will now cast her horoscope. But you must tell her that an infinite amount of hard labour, calculations, and tremendous re-checking. Keep her waiting. She will barely be able to wait out the week, and within the allotted amount of time she will telephone you. 'Is my horoscope ready?'

It is, you having meanwhile used your typewriter, ten pieces of paper, and a horoscope partly copied from one of the more obscure magazines. That is to say you will not copy it quite exactly but use only the technical positions of the stars and considerable fancy of your own. If you have any trepidations just check one astrology magazine against the other and you will come to note that no one astrologer agrees with the other; therefore, why should you, another astrologer, agree with all the rest? And upon these ten accompanying sheets you will typewrite just exactly everything the stars command her to do day by day for the next three months. We sincerely hope that you will make the stars show the least bit of common ordinary horse sense. After all, she will be following a typewritten list of your instructions for three months!

And a Last Word

MANNERS FOR THE GUEST

The best guest is the best guesser. He puts clue and clue together to figure out what his hosts' expect of him, then does what is expected as if it were the very thing he wanted most.

As more and more rules give way to more and more ad-lib etiquette, the guest's guesses are more and more difficult. One hostess may be irritated if he does not appear on the stroke of the prescribed hour; another may be upset (and only half-dressed) if he is less than fifteen minutes late.

One host may boil if he mixes his own drinks; another may think their party's a failure if people leave before 4 am, where another will think their guests are planning to move in if they aren't out of the house by midnight.

Thus the guest's job is to read minds, assess habits and operate on a social-radar system super-sensitive to his host's hopes and plans. Since the host's job is to do the same, in reverse, the guest cannot be completely flaccid: he has to have some wishes so his host can grant them; he has to have some preferences so his host can cater to them. The delicate part of the guest's role comes in adapting his wishes and preferences to the host's own wishes and preferences – and to the host's ability to provide for them.